The Smart Job Search

A Guide
to Proven Methods
for Finding
a Great Job

Marc L. Makos

HD Publishing
Boston, Masschusetts

About the Author

Marc L. Makos is president of Smart Résumés in Boston, Massachusetts. His company puts together the packages clients need to successfully compete for the best jobs. Mr. Makos looks forward to any correspondence you may be inclined to write. He may be reached as follows:

Marc L. Makos
c/o HD Publishing
P.O. Box 2171
Boston, MA 02106

Mr. Makos will have his next title, **Résumés for The Smart Job Search**, published by HD Publishing in January, 1992. In this book recruiters, employment agencies and others will analyze résumés and offer advice(adding certain skills, specific areas of education needed, job opportunities, etc.).

Warning—Disclaimer

Trademarks

Trademarked names appear in various parts of this book, particularly in the chapter of résumé examples. Instead of listing the names and entities that own these trademarks or insert a trademark symbol every time the trademarked name is mentioned, the publisher and author state that the trademarked names are used only for editorial purposes and to the benefit of the trademark owner with absolutely no intention of infringing upon that trademark.

Library of Congress Cataloging–in–Publication Data

Makos, Marc L.
    The smart job search : a guide to proven methods for finding a
great job / Marc L. Makos.
            p.   cm.
    Includes index.
    ISBN 0–9630394–8–2 : $18.95
    1. Job hunting.
    2. Résumés (Employment)
    3. Cover letters.
    4. Employment interviewing.
    I. Title.
HF5382.7.M34   1991   91–31232
650. 14--dc20   CIP

1st Edition

Printed in the United States of America

Published by:
HD Publishing
Post Office Box 2171
Boston, MA 02106 U.S.A.

Table of Contents

you. You'll learn to write the résumé that works best for your needs. You'll learn how to make the best of the job interview. You'll use those skills that are important to you and discard those which either don't sell in today's market or limit your career growth.

Are you satisfied with your career? If your answer is yes, allow this book to add depth to your job search. If you answered no, use this book to define your goals, package your skills and abilities, present yourself to the marketplace and get the best possible job.

Perhaps you're facing a difficult job market. Unemployment is rising and your industry is facing massive layoffs. Even so, remember that companies need skilled employees at every level and at all times. Employees retire. Some people move. Others find personal reasons for leaving a company. The point is that if you can identify your talents and show those talents to the marketplace you'll find a satisfying job.

Similarly, if you cannot identify your real talents, if your résumé is not powerful and you cannot make contacts as you need them, your job campaign will be second or third rate.

Consider that résumé readers first skim over a pile of applicants(a one-inch thick pile of résumés). They've developed skills to separate the good from the ugly(please, never lose a job because of smudges, typos and a poor layout). This weeding out process takes about 30 seconds per résumé, or less! With such a short time to sell the reader you've got to ensure the following:

1. That your résumé is flawless and easy to read.
2. That your résumé is perceived to be better than the rest of the competition in the pile.
3. That the résumé is convincing, impressive and relevant.
4. That the reader wants to meet you.

When your résumé has all of these components you'll help yourself get to the next stage: the interview itself. If your résumé lacks these components, you'll lose out on many opportunities.

This book will show you how not to lose all of the opportunities and possibilities that exist.

Every aspect of your job search will be explained thoroughly. This book will help you understand how the parts of a job search are interrelated. Fail at your research and you'll hurt your interview. Choose the wrong references and you'll lose some offers. Go unprepared to your interview and you won't be invited back. Create a poor résumé and you'll have to settle for less.

Why settle for less? Add to your skills. Develop those skills that get you more in life.

More money.
More skills.
More job benefits.
More excitement.
More out of life!

A note of caution is in order. Some chapters of this book may not seem to apply to you. Or, you may only follow the first parts of this book and then strike out for job offers. Don't read only part of this book. You'll likely hurt your chances for the greatest success.

Read the book thoroughly. Read through it once before filling out any of the exercises. Grasp the fundamentals of the text before analyzing the details of the worksheets.

What if you're a bank executive and you want to be a tennis coach? What if you're an engineer and you want to run your own dairy farm? Use the principles in this book to change careers wisely. The same methods of research and presentation will assist every situation.

Combine what you are interested in with what you're able to do. The bank executive will use his computer skills to write programs analyzing the swing of a tennis pro. The engineer will use her skills to redesign the system for milking the cows, increasing production and turning the enterprise profitable.

And don't think that unless you change careers you'll be stuck with the same job title or profession.

Consider a legal secretary. Yes, jobs abound in law firms. But what of the law office in a bank? How about the legal office for the international shipping company? Could working for a judge, an audit firm, a housing development agency or a private consulting firm be possible? Working in all these situations is possible. Research is the key.

Research will prepare you for the interview. This book is unique in its presentation regarding those tough interview questions. By putting in the effort of answering those sample questions, you'll shine at the interview. You'll prove that you are the best candidate, most able and best qualified to do the job. You are not left alone with those questions. For each question, you are given the highlights and hidden meanings from the interviewers' perspective. You'll also have a sample answer for each question.

You will learn all the important elements of a successful job search. How to research an industry. How to research a company. Putting together the most powerful résumé. Preparing for and succeeding at the job interview. Following through on every lead. Building a network of contacts. And accepting the best job.

Those are the skills you will learn with this book. If you want to understand what you need to get that dream job, this book is right for you.

With technologies changing so fast, it's what are called the "lifetime learners" who'll get ahead in the future. You'll learn to excel at new technologies. You'll be flexible enough to work in many environments, volunteering at every turn. Part-time, full-time, consulting, temporary assignments and telecommuting are just some of the ways you may create the best job for you. If you desire to, you can be the maker of your work life.

The education you received yesterday may not be as important today. Your job ten years ago may be irrelevant because the job has become obsolete. Only what you can do today and in the future counts.

Those individuals who rest on the accomplishments of the past, no matter how exemplary, may find offers lacking in the future. You've picked up this book to accept the challenges of a better future. Use this book. Many will find they can't afford not to.

You'll learn to show those basic values that carry over to a future profession. You'll express values(those which make up your past and will determine your future) in terms of:

    Stability
    Reliability
    Experience
    Leadership
    Motivation
    Adaptation, and perhaps most importantly,
    Capacity to Learn

These qualities are self-defined. If you look to a counselor, a friend or family member to define these qualities for you, beware the outcome.

Take a look around you at family and friends. Come up with a quick résumé snapshot for each of them. Some may have more education. Some may have less. Some may have changed careers frequently and advanced steadily. Others may have worked in the same company for twenty years, enjoying or putting up with the same job over the last ten of those years. Each of them has defined their qualifications for the job market. Their job market.

Their self-definitions can greatly affect your own search. They may help you. More often, though, their honest efforts will only have a negative impact on you. If you understand why, you'll be able to listen to their advice while still doing what's best for you.

When someone gives advice on a new purchase(i.e. a new car), suggestions are based on what they know and personal preferences. So too with the job search. The problem is that their opinions are based on their own experiences and what has happened to them. Their definition of self-worth will totally influence how they help you. This help can be triply dangerous.

First, they may have accepted a job three levels below their qualifications. The result is a self-appraisal that is below what is possible.

Second, one or more of their qualifications may be held in greater esteem. For example, you may have one year less education than your friend. They may therefore suggest to you that you should accept a job one level below their own. This suggestion may not take into account the vast skills and experience that you have which they do not share(an individual finds it easier to ignore his or her own shortcomings when planning your career!).

Third, you may agree with their assessment. We are conditioned as a people to put numbers on everything. Is a more expensive house a better house? Always? Is a private school better than a public school you pay taxes for? Is the child better off in the private school, even if her parents visit her twice a year and forget her birthday?

Many people will have their best intentions set for you. Set your own best intentions. Use this book to put together an objective analysis of yourself. Sell yourself on yourself. Remember, all experience counts.

You will not get the right job unless you know what the right job for you is. Give yourself small goals and achieve them. Make deadlines and beat them. Let this book help you set your own terms and prosper!

"Why Do I Need A Résumé?"

The résumé is a written document. Writing is a key part to many jobs in the current marketplace. Your résumé identifies whether or not you possess this key trait. Your résumé is your autobiography. Be proud of it.

As said in the introduction, you will always want to be aware of and add to your skills. The normal worker may change positions as many as ten times in their lives. You should understand that constantly appraising your abilities and being able to present them is of utmost importance to your career. A résumé helps form that appraisal in your mind.

If you change jobs as many as ten times, a constant reappraisal is crucial. Defining and refining your abilities and accomplishments will better equip you for the next job. Keeping up to date on developments in your field is important. Your résumé will help identify weaknesses as well as strengths(to you, not to the employer).

Job changes may be planned or unplanned. If you are fired or part of a company layoff, if your company relocates or reorganizes to your detriment, preparedness will be your best ally. Simply put, part of success in the future will be a ready plan for your next career.

Having a résumé is a great way to organize your thoughts. The résumé is your representation after you've left the prospective employer. This representation is important. The employer may pass your résumé on to others in the department.

You may be considered for positions that you haven't applied for. Your identity is carried forward by this piece of paper. Don't do yourself a disservice by putting only a cursory effort into your résumé.

Throughout this book, you'll be given advice for approaching various segments of the job market. The advice may, at times, seem out of place. It is not. The whole job search process is interrelated. Each lead, each method of research will give you material which will affect other efforts. For example, a suggestion may direct a refinement or change to an important interview or research assignment.

Let's consider a seemingly out of place piece of advice for a moment. We'll consider two hints for responding to a Sunday advertisement.

1. Send your résumé out the following mid-week, either Wednesday or Thursday.
2. If you haven't heard a response within one week of sending the material, send another résumé at that time.
3. In each case, send a cover letter with the résumé.

You might want to disregard this advice. If so, answer these questions. If you send your résumé immediately, along with everyone else, how will your résumé arrive? It will arrive as one of many. If the prospective employer reviews this stack of résumés(yours is 27th in a stack of 55), are you assured an advantage over the competition?

Now, let's say those 55 have been narrowed down to 5. At that time your résumé arrives. The employer has already gone through the weeding out process. Five résumés remain that stood out from the rest. When your résumé arrives it will be judged against the remaining 5, not the original 55. This book shows you how to compete only with the best. Be one of the finalists when your résumé arrives.

The decision is yours. Do you want to compete with 54 résumés or with 5? Granted, the 5 will be the best. But the 5 best are exactly what you want to compete with. Don't get screened out of the process simply because the employer is tired and inattentive when your résumé gets to the top of the pile.

That advice doesn't say what is on a great résumé, but it does show what a great résumé will do for you.

A résumé will allow you to present yourself in the best possible light. Equally important, though, you'll come to understand where you have repetitive problems in your career. You'll see if personal factors have contributed to a slowing of advancement. You'll learn how to define a career where satisfaction can be achieved.

Just as you develop new skills as an adult, so too you develop new interests and abilities, new hobbies. Use this book to determine whether you have what it takes to earn a profit from your hobby. Writing a résumé will give you insights into the skills you have and help you determine whether you should pursue self–employment.

Once you determine for yourself what an ideal position is, you'll use your résumé to your benefit. Once you've got the job, you'll help the company help you. Companies find it easier to train their own staff. It is cheaper for the company to promote from within. You'll excel and contribute. You'll develop qualities that allow the company to send you up the company ladder of success. Rewriting your résumé every year not only tells you where you've been, but helps define where you should go next.

If you identify every skill you have and write them all on your résumé, you are offering each of those skills to a prospective employer. What if you hate to do something that you do well? This book will show you how to express other skills that will impress even the most difficult interviewer. You've got too many fine skills to have to present those that you do not want to make part of your job.

Even when you do not write the following words on your résumé, consider their impact. You may think about a company and a job offer in these terms:

- I want to meet new people on a regular basis.
- I don't mind spending time in an office but there should be opportunities for field work.
- I have become so excited about my hobby. I want it to play a role in my job.
- I don't like having others plan my day. I am a self-starter and would like to be recognized as one.
- I'm always chosen to lead the group. I want this to continue.
- I've volunteered for every new project. I want to be able to join special projects in a new company.
- I would like to deal with people my own age.
- I've always enjoyed working with active senior citizen groups.
- I really want to work in a non-smoking environment.
- I want to become friends with my co-workers, socializing with them on weekends.
- I want to keep business and social lives separate.
- I really thrive in a fact-paced environment.
- I need tranquility, a place where I can spend time alone.
- I have definite ideas about the length of my commute.

Now, list five of your own needs:

1.
2.
3.
4.
5.

A job or a career is more than a paycheck. A working environment has to satisfy you on many different levels. Know what your needs are. Satisfy those needs. Learn to slant your résumé to your own interests.

You have to set a clear focus on what you want. You'll have to plan your strategies carefully. Strategies will include presenting yourself on paper and in person as best as possible.

You'll become a great salesperson and a great negotiator. You'll research your markets thoroughly and be prepared to move decisively when opportunities arise.

A résumé offers immediate support to all other parts of your job search. The résumé refreshes your memory. It also refreshes the memory of the employer.

If you've recently lost your job, whether by layoff or getting fired, use the résumé writing process to rebuild your self-esteem. Lacking a clear plan of what you want in your next career and facing rejections at the same time is altogether disheartening. Don't rush into the marketplace a day after the layoff. Rushing back to the market may actually hurt you a great deal. Emotionally, yes. Financially, most definitely.

Consider when you absolutely have to have a job. If you have cash or a savings account, stocks, bonds or other assets, you may find enough resources to survive a month, six months or more without having a job. If you'll lose your home if you don't find a job in ten days, you're in a very different situation. The longer you can prepare yourself the better off you'll be.

Assume we have two people accepting jobs. The first begins working on January 1st. The second begins on April 1st. Both will do precisely the same job and should earn the same salary. Both lost their last jobs on December 15th.

Call our January 1st example Ben.

Call our April 1st example Mary.

Ben became scared and accepted a job offer, starting January 1st, at a salary of $25,000.

Mary thoroughly researched her industry and the companies that were best positioned for growth. The research, résumé writing, interviews and follow-ups took three months. Mary accepted her job, starting March 1st, at a salary of $30,000.

For the calendar year ending December 31st, each will earn precisely the same amount of money, $25,000. (Assume benefits are identical.) Now, assume that benefits remain the same and that each receives the same 10% raise every January 1st for the next four years. How do our candidates, each with identical skills and jobs, succeed over our time frame?

Ben(January 1st at $25,000.):

Year 1	$25,000.
Year 2	$27,500.
Year 3	$30,250.
Year 4	$33,275.
Year 5	$36,602.50

Total Received: $152,627.50

Mary(March 1st at $30,000.):

Year 1	$25,000.
Year 2	$33,000.
Year 3	$36,300.
Year 4	$39,930.
Year 5	$43,923.

Total Received: $178,153.00

A difference of $25,525.50! Granted, we cannot expect conditions to remain identical for five years. But, we suggest the extra $25K+ for Mary is lower than what the actual discrepancy will be. In all likelihood, Mary will be ahead of Ben by far more than the $25,525.50. Here's why.

Ben has spent two weeks out of work. In that time, he's had to recover from the shock of job loss. He's had to analyze his skills, develop and produce a résumé, research companies, respond to advertisements, schedule interviews and accept a job offer. I sincerely doubt whether Ben could have accomplished all of the above to the best of his ability and in his own best interests.

Mary recovered from the job loss. She spent the Christmas holiday realizing the true gifts of life. The holidays brought friends, relatives and acquaintances together. Mary expressed interest in other opinions regarding the job market and possible choices for a new career. January came. Mary spent the whole month researching industries and companies, attending informational interviews and creating a powerful résumé. The first week of February continued much like the month before. She did, however, set up two job interviews. The second week of February brought seven interviews, evenly spaced out over the week. The third week brought follow-up interviews with two companies. Both companies made offers. Mary accepted one of them. The final week of February was a busy time for Mary. She wrote to all those involved in her job search. She thanked each of them. She did not send them a form letter. Each letter expressed her appreciation for the particular help given. Finally, Mary poured a hot cup of tea and reviewed the literature she'd requested and received from her new employer.

What differentiates our two job seekers? More than likely, job satisfaction. Though Mary will earn $178,153 over five years, Ben will probably do worse than expected. If Ben quits the job and changes jobs just once more in the five year period, with a month between old and new jobs this time, total earnings will drop another $2500.

Even more probable, Ben will become dissatisfied over and over again. In five years he may have 3 different jobs, with weeks out of work between each. Performance may be a problem. (After all, Ben doesn't like his job.) Raises and promotions may be reduced or not given at all.

Meanwhile, Mary thrives and prospers. The ultimate difference in wages could easily top $50,000.

Don't rush your campaign. Set up a schedule for yourself. Give yourself lists of things to do. Study. Research, research and research some more. Know your strengths. Expect rejections. Make your own success.

Use your résumé to help you keep a grip on reality. The résumé will give you a quick recap of all you've done. Don't use the résumé to remind yourself of what you haven't accomplished. Instead, use the résumé as a tool to promote your current abilities. And use it as a resource in defining those skills you need to learn so that you'll succeed in the future.

Companies only want to make money. They are loyal to the bottom line. You want to make as much money as you desire. Use the résumé to combine both needs.

Make money for them. Save money for them. Your résumé is often the first thing that identifies you with the employer. Quality sells. Your résumé quality will sell you.

Do you already have a résumé of quality? Are you sure?

Are your thoughts poorly organized? Are your sentences too long? Do you use punctuation incorrectly? Do you spell some words incorrectly? Do you abbreviate where you shouldn't or use technical terms not common throughout the industry? Do you have a message to tell but are unsure how to tell it? This book gives you a step-by-step formula for achieving the best success possible.

Once you've got a great résumé, what do you do with it? A great résumé may help you in more ways than simply getting a paying job. Package a powerful résumé to:

1. Give to your banker to prove those qualities needed for getting a loan.
2. Show your civic organization that you've got what it takes to head a project.
3. Qualify yourself for volunteer work at a museum or hospital.
4. Remind yourself of the next steps you'll need to take in order to advance your skills.
5. State your worth with no apologies.

Your résumé may affect the rest of your working life. You must understand that it is an important document. Content is important. Format is important also.

How does it look? After you've read this book and completed all exercises, refer to the last page of this book, which is entitled 'Resources'. You will find other resources available that will add to your job search and working life.

Give yourself enough time to identify exactly what you want. If an impending layoff is at hand, spend the week or month beforehand preparing yourself for the job hunt. You'll find it difficult to make changes immediately. The only thing you can change immediately is your attitude. Have a positive attitude towards personal success.

Now, move on the the next chapter, 'Focusing on Strengths'. Add clarity to your vision.

Focusing on Strengths

There are aspects about a job that are important to you. You may like the people. Being connected to a particular company may make you feel proud. The job may include no travelling, allowing you to spend more time with family. The job may require you to attend intensive training courses, etc..

All of the above are aspects of a job. Something not part of your physical work may actually rank very highly for why you'll love the job.

For example, let's assume a job offers flexible work hours. Suppose you're also allowed to spend 25% of your work week at home. Let's say you're a single mother with two small children. What would these terms mean to you? Do you like the sound of the job? If you say yes, realize that we haven't even identified the job or its responsibilities.

Without knowing what the job is, think about what the company making the offer finds acceptable:

1. 'The company respects my responsibilities as a single mother.'
2. 'I can attend school functions and help develop the talents of my children.'
3. 'The company can see how I contribute by the results I produce.'
4. 'The company does not have a "punch the timeclock" mentality.'

Think about what the company thinks about this mother:

1. 'She is a responsible mother and worker.'
2. 'She will be counted on not to take advantage of the flexible work hours.'
3. 'She will supervise herself.'
4. 'She will be assigned a project and complete it.'
5. 'She'll use the company as a resource, not as a means to a paycheck.'
6. 'She is disciplined and won't need to be disciplined.'

You'll certainly have your own reasons for job satisfaction.

Perhaps you love to work outdoors. You may find happiness working all day long in front of a computer terminal. Or you might be very happy supporting one person in an organization. Finally, maybe you want to read all the product literature that comes into an office.

However you approach the job search, you must first decide which things make you happy and how they'll contribute to your success. You're guaranteed that if you hate what you do but do it for the paycheck, you'll know many things. For example:

1. You won't want to get up in the morning.
2. You won't want to come back from lunch.
3. You won't be as concerned with your appearance.
4. Good health won't be as important to you. Being sick will give you time away from the job.
5. During vacations, you'll spend time thinking about the job and how you don't want to go back to it.
6. You'll probably quit instead of trying for a promotion.
7. You'll continue to have bills all your life.
8. You'll settle for less of a home, lesser quality possessions and less time with family and friends.
9. You'll have less responsibility.
10. You'll have an overbearing supervisor.
11. You'll resent successful people, limiting friendships and business contacts.
12. You'll get old and have a limited budget.
13. You'll die, with many plans unfulfilled.

Contrast that analysis with these traits if you love your job:

1. You'll sleep well.
2. Waking will come more easily, often without an alarm clock.
3. You'll smile more.
4. You'll get to work on schedule or earlier.
5. People at work will be glad to see you.
6. You'll be given more to do. You'll learn more, achieve more, receive praise, gain recognition and promotions.
7. You'll come back from vacation totally refreshed, excited to learn what has happened while you were away.
8. You'll earn more money.
9. You'll have a better house, finer clothes and more interest in family and friends.
10. Successful people will want you as a friend or associate.
11. You'll get old, have more savings and a higher pension. You'll have more interests and more financial means to pursue them.
12. You'll die, probably with less illness and disability, at an advanced age. Many plans will have been fulfilled.

Yes, you have to earn a living. Consider the principles outlined in this book as a method for achieving a better living.

Complete the following exercise.

You've walked in to your dream job one month ago today. Later tonight, you'll speak with enthusiasm to family and friends about the past month. Tell them three things you do and why you do them. Then, tell them three things that happened to you unexpectedly and why.

Examples I do these things:	Your Example I do these things:
1. I do the monthly budget report on the computer because I design the best charts.	1.

2. I type all correspondence for the   2.
Vice President because my work is
consistently error-free.

3. I do the presentations to customers   3.
because I'm the best public speaker.

This happened unexpectedly: Unexpectedly:

1. I won an award since I had the   1.
highest overall sales figure in the office.

2. I was selected to lead a project to   2.
carry out my ideas for reorganizing
the office.

3. I was made manager of the deli.   3.
They said customers really liked me.

Balance your dreams with the skills you have. This does not mean you'll give up your dreams. Instead, you'll identify all your skills and learn of other skills you'll need to fulfill those dreams. Research will be the key. Then you'll have the basis for proving your qualifications and worth for the job you seek.

Now, it's time to look back at your work and personal life. You will identify successes you've had. More importantly, you'll explain and analyze why these successes give you pride.

Note: Sometimes a book such as this one is read at a low point in people's lives. Your job may have turned sour. Perhaps you were fired or laid-off. You're self-esteem may be at a very low point. You may find it difficult to identify any successes.

Still, you absolutely do have successes in life. You'll be asked to identify ten of them. Even if you can't think of one success, read each of the questions and reflect on your own life. Think of past work history. Think of schooling, family, friends, community organizations, etc.. Dedicate a good portion of time to this exercise. Complete it in solitude or whatever privacy you can find. You'll be able to identify ten successes.

For example, are you a member of the PTA? Do you attend church services? Did you help on a Sunday supper? Have you coached little league? Do you have children? How were they raised? Were you ever promoted? Did you ever write for the school newspaper? Did you ever paint or sculpt? Did you win a prize for your creation? Did you win any other awards for anything you've done in life? Did you ever plant a garden?

If you reconsider all you've done during your career and lifetime, you'll discover ten proud moments of accomplishment. Just take your time in discovering them. (By the way, career can be defined as volunteer work, a year of co-op during college, 30 years at one firm, etc..)

Now, it is time to identify the ten successes. For now, stay with work-related successes. For each, answer the questions listed. Your answers may be brief or may encompass a paragraph or more.

As you fill this section out, remember that employers will hire you if they get more value from you than your cost to them. Value, though, covers many areas. You may provide much needed solutions to their problems. You may be effective at cost-cutting measures. You may be able to organize a department so that it will run less expensively. You may be able to create a safe environment where only the best talent will want to work. All of these values are profitable to a business. Think of all your values as you work on this exercise.

Now, relax and begin.

Success Number One

1. What was your success? What are you proud of?

   _____

   _____

2. Why did this success happen to you? How did you get involved?

   _____

   _____

3. Did anything or anyone get in the way? How did you deal with obstacles?

_____

_____

4. How did this success affect the company? Does the company earn more money because of it? How much? Did you save money? How much? Do people, including yourself, work better now because of this? How?

_____

_____

5. What year(s) did this happen?

_____

Success Number Two

1. What was your success? What are you proud of?

_____

_____

2. Why did this success happen to you? How did you get involved?

_____

_____

3. Did anything or anyone get in the way? How did you deal with obstacles?

_____

_____

4. How did this success affect the company? Does the company earn more money because of it? How much? Did you save money? How much? Do people, including yourself, work better now because of this? How?

_____

5. What year(s) did this happen?

_____

Success Number Three

1. What was your success? What are you proud of?

_____

_____

2. Why did this success happen to you? How did you get involved?

_____

_____

3. Did anything or anyone get in the way? How did you deal with obstacles?

_____

_____

4. How did this success affect the company? Does the company earn more money because of it? How much? Did you save money? How much? Do people, including yourself, work better now because of this? How?

_____

_____

5. What year(s) did this happen?

_____

Success Number Four

1. What was your success? What are you proud of?

_____

_____

2. Why did this success happen to you? How did you get involved?

_____

3. Did anything or anyone get in the way? How did you deal with obstacles?

_____

_____

4. How did this success affect the company? Does the company earn more money because of it? How much? Did you save money? How much? Do people, including yourself, work better now because of this? How?

_____

_____

5. What year(s) did this happen?

_____

Success Number Five

1. What was your success? What are you proud of?

_____

_____

2. Why did this success happen to you? How did you get involved?

_____

_____

3. Did anything or anyone get in the way? How did you deal with obstacles?

_____

_____

4. How did this success affect the company? Does the company earn more money because of it? How much? Did you save money? How much? Do people, including yourself, work better now because of this? How?

_____

_____

5. What year(s) did this happen?

_____

Success Number Six

1. What was your success? What are you proud of?

   _____

   _____

2. Why did this success happen to you? How did you get involved?

   _____

   _____

3. Did anything or anyone get in the way? How did you deal with obstacles?

   _____

   _____

4. How did this success affect the company? Does the company earn more money because of it? How much? Did you save money? How much? Do people, including yourself, work better now because of this? How?

   _____

   _____

5. What year(s) did this happen?

   _____

Success Number Seven

1. What was your success? What are you proud of?

   _____

   _____

2. Why did this success happen to you? How did you get involved?

   _____

   _____

3. Did anything or anyone get in the way? How did you deal with obstacles?

_____

_____

4. How did this success affect the company? Does the company earn more money because of it? How much? Did you save money? How much? Do people, including yourself, work better now because of this? How?

_____

_____

5. What year(s) did this happen?

_____

Success Number Eight

1. What was your success? What are you proud of?

_____

_____

2. Why did this success happen to you? How did you get involved?

_____

_____

3. Did anything or anyone get in the way? How did you deal with obstacles?

_____

_____

4. How did this success affect the company? Does the company earn more money because of it? How much? Did you save money? How much? Do people, including yourself, work better now because of this? How?

_____

_____

5. What year(s) did this happen?

_____

Success Number Nine

1. What was your success? What are you proud of?

_____

_____

2. Why did this success happen to you? How did you get involved?

_____

_____

3. Did anything or anyone get in the way? How did you deal with obstacles?

_____

_____

4. How did this success affect the company? Does the company earn more money because of it? How much? Did you save money? How much? Do people, including yourself, work better now because of this? How?

_____

_____

5. What year(s) did this happen?

_____

Success Number Ten

1. What was your success? What are you proud of?

_____

_____

2. Why did this success happen to you? How did you get involved?

_____

_____

3. Did anything or anyone get in the way? How did you deal with obstacles?

_____

4. How did this success affect the company? Does the company earn more money because of it? How much? Did you save money? How much? Do people, including yourself, work better now because of this? How?

_____

_____

5. What year(s) did this happen?

_____

Your résumé builds on these strengths. You want the prospective employer to know these strengths. Realize the employer will want information from you. This information, though, should only be presented as being beneficial to them.

You've identified ten successes in your career. Now you should begin the process of writing short, bold statements that show results. When you turn each of the ten successes into powerful statements you've gone a good distance towards a great résumé.

You'll include the following in each of the power statements:

1. A strong action verb.
   'Created...'
   'Built...'
   'Targeted...'

2. An identification of the success.

3. The results in specific terms such as dollars saved or efficiency gained.

You've answered five questions for each of the ten successes. The power statements will come from these answers. Power statements average about 8 to 15 words per sentence.

Here are two examples for you to consider:

Success Example Number One

1. What was your success? What are you proud of?

I was group leader in my department for a quality control
project.

2. Why did this success happen to you? How did you get
    involved?

My manager asked me to do it. He said I always take extra
effort with my job and said he needed the same kind of effort
to get the project completed.

3. Did anything or anyone get in the way? How did you deal
    with obstacles?

Each department had to have a team made up of 5 people. I
had 2 great people volunteer. The other 3 positions needed
filling and I wanted certain people for those slots. I sat with
those people and explained what management wanted to
accomplish with the project, how our department would
benefit and how pleased senior management would be with
the 5 of us.

4. How did this success affect the company? Does the
    company earn more money because of it? How much?
    Did you save money? How much? Do people, including
    yourself, work better now because of this? How?

First, we finished ahead of schedule and ahead of all other
groups. Within 3 months we initiated 3 of our proposals.
Customer statements went out faster. We even cut back the
production cycle on the system by 6 hours. We figured we
saved the company about $30,000 annually.

5. What year(s) did this happen?

1989

Power Statement:

• Selected to put together team for quality control project. Oversaw efforts of 5 team members. Completed project ahead of schedule and enacted 3 proposals which saved $30,000 annually.

Success Example Number Two

1. What was your success? What are you proud of?

I'm most proud of the fact that I just do a good job.

2. Why did this success happen to you? How did you get involved?

Because I'm a good worker. Well, every time I'm asked to do something I just do it. I get the stuff done on time and without errors.

3. Did anything or anyone get in the way? How did you deal with obstacles?

The guy down the hall tried to screw up my day by giving me little things to do. Trivial things, but I think he was jealous because I got along so well with my boss. One day, I told him I'd be more than happy to continue doing things for him but that my work for my boss was being affected. I told him if he cleared these things through my boss I'd be happy to carry them out. Since then, he hasn't bothered me.

4. How did this success affect the company? Does the company earn more money because of it? How much? Did you save money? How much? Do people, including yourself, work better now because of this? How?

<u>Well, I get jobs back to my boss a day faster now. She can catch</u>
<u>an earlier train because my preparatory work is now done</u>
<u>earlier. I don't know about any dollars saved.</u>

5. What year(s) did this happen?

<u>1990</u>

Power Statement:

• Maintained high level of support to manager, changing working environment to process documents 25% more quickly. Allowed manager to respond to clients faster.

Now, you should review your answers to the ten successes. For each success, you'll write a power statement. Follow the examples presented, but write power statements that truly reflect your own talents.

Your Power Statement from Success Number One

•

Your Power Statement from Success Number Two

•

Your Power Statement from Success Number Three

•

Your Power Statement from Success Number Four

*

Your Power Statement from Success Number Five

*

Your Power Statement from Success Number Six

*

Your Power Statement from Success Number Seven

*

Your Power Statement from Success Number Eight

*

Your Power Statement from Success Number Nine

*

Your Power Statement from Success Number Ten

*

Don't worry if some sentences are 5 words or 18 words long. Your objective is to make clear your value to a new employer.

You have other values to an employer. Some may find their way onto the résumé. Others will not, but may play an important role in your research or in an interview. We'll call these 'life values'.

What you can do certainly is important. But who you are is also vitally important.

Compare these two individuals. Call them Susan and David. You will have to hire one of them.

Susan graduated from a prestigious college. She knows four types of computer languages. Susan is a member of a private club.

David attended college but did not graduate. He knows three computer languages. David is not a member of a private club.

Hire one of these people right now. Your choice is: _____

Now, let's give you added 'inside information' about our two candidates.

Susan was caught cheating more than once in college. Her family pulled strings to get Susan her diploma. She knows the fundamentals of the four languages but is not an expert in any of them. Her work is sloppy. Associates don't like working on a project with Susan because she thrives on taking all the credit. Susan arrived at your interview 5 minutes late and didn't apologize. She looked at the floor when shaking your hand and asked to borrow a pen to write some notes. Later, Susan relaxes at the club. Family money of $5,000 per year entitles Susan to belong to the club.

David maintained high grades while in college. He has a spouse and two children and found attending school full-time just wasn't possible. David continues to attend school part-time. He should have his degree in about two more years. David is considered an expert in two of the three computer languages he knows. He is always asked to be part of a team. Everyone knows David shares in the success of the group and he doesn't try to take full credit. David has arrived at the interview location 10 minutes early and checked his appearance. He has gone through a mock run of the interview in his mind. When meeting, David looks you squarely in the eye and says "I'm David Saunders and I'm very glad to meet you". David has a broad smile and his words were genuine. You find out at the end of the interview that David will be starting his first night as a board member of the PTA that evening.

Now hire your future working partner:_____

Of course your skills are important. The following items are equally important:

1. Your smile and sincerity.
2. Your handshake.
3. Your sense of humor and perceived intelligence.
4. Your enthusiasm about the job.
5. Whether you can make eye contact.
6. Whether you can relax.
7. Whether you can work as part of a team.
8. Whether you are a progressive thinker and willing to learn.
9. Most importantly, whether the person doing the hiring likes you.

These 'life values' will help get you the job. They'll help get you the promotions. They'll affect salary and bonuses. These life values will give you more happiness in your life.

You should now be ready to identify your own life values. These values may include volunteer work you do, organizations you are a member of, school functions you take part in, hobbies you pursue, research or writing you do, etc..

Are you ready to answer more questions? (Whether or not you feel it, give an enthusiastic yes!)

Life Value Number One

1. What do you do outside of the career that makes you happy?

   _____

   _____

   _____

2. How did you get involved with this?

   _____

   _____

   _____

3. Do you make contributions to it? Do you write, paint, create, build or make preparations for this? What are your contributions?

   _____

   _____

   _____

4. Are there certain skills you needed to have before doing this? Did you attend classes, workshops or anything else to help you?

   _____

   _____

   _____

5. How does this affect your life? Have you found other things to do because of it? Do you participate in team events? Do you have more friends now? Who are they?

   _____

   _____

   _____

Life Value Number Two

1. What do you do outside of the career that makes you happy?

_____

_____

_____

2. How did you get involved with this?

_____

_____

_____

3. Do you make contributions to it? Do you write, paint, create, build or make preparations for this? What are your contributions?

_____

_____

_____

4. Are there certain skills you needed to have before doing this? Did you attend classes, workshops or anything else to help you?

_____

_____

_____

5. How does this affect your life? Have you found other things to do because of it? Do you participate in team events? Do you have more friends now? Who are they?

_____

_____

_____

Life Value Number Three

1. What do you do outside of the career that makes you happy?

    _____

    _____

    _____

2. How did you get involved with this?

    _____

    _____

    _____

3. Do you make contributions to it? Do you write, paint, create, build or make preparations for this? What are your contributions?

    _____

    _____

    _____

4. Are there certain skills you needed to have before doing this? Did you attend classes, workshops or anything else to help you?

    _____

    _____

    _____

5. How does this affect your life? Have you found other things to do because of it? Do you participate in team events? Do you have more friends now? Who are they?

    _____

    _____

    _____

You may certainly write about more than three life values. Simply continue the process on a separate sheet of paper.

Quick Tip

What do you do if your previous work and life experiences don't encompass all the qualities needed to get a certain position? First, research, research and research some more. If you feel a certain job may demand more skills than you currently have, complete the following exercise:

1. Determine, exactly, the skills you have that seem to be required for this position.

1._____
2._____
3._____
4._____
5._____

2. Determine, exactly, those skills you feel you do not have seeming to be required for this position.

1._____
2._____
3._____
4._____
5._____

3. Determine how you would get any of the missing skills that you seem to need for this position.

1._____
2._____
3._____
4._____
5._____

4. Determine, exactly, other skills not required that you would bring to the position while you were getting the skills determined in step #3.

1._____
2._____
3._____
4._____
5._____

Remember, if you get the job with the promise of adding skills, fulfilling those skill requirements is the complete responsibility of one person. You! The company may assist you, but you should prove your value by accomplishing what you set out to do. And on or before schedule.

Success follows success. Volunteer for special assignments. Learn more about your product than anyone else. Contribute your skills to a team. You'll continue on an upward journey through the organization.

Visualization

Visualize yourself reviewing your career highlights with a friend. Using the strengths you've already defined or new highlights that you'll be adding to the list, tell the friend at least ten instances where you:

1. Had a problem or a challenge.
2. Took action on that problem or challenge.
3. Achieved a positive result. Identify the result in terms of its benefit to the company or to your own life.

You may think this exercise is simply a repetition of previous exercises. It is except for one very important point. You are not writing anything down. You are simply telling your friend a story. You are clear and precise. You are proud and confident.

Why should you do this? The reason is simple. You'll want to be able to easily express your accomplishments. You'll be relaxed and secure with a friend. Visually picture your friend when highlighting the proud moments of your life. Then, substitute another friend for the one you've imagined. Tell your story again. Next, substitute the face of a stranger and tell your story again.

Continue to substitute new faces of strangers until you feel comfortable telling your story. Substitute faces of young women and men, fat men smoking cigars, skinny woman with crooked teeth, etc.. When you feel at ease telling your successes to any of these real and imagined people, you'll be prepared for the interview.

Many times you won't see the interviewer until the actual interview itself. Being relaxed and confident are important selling features. Your rehearsals will have prepared you for whomever is facing you across the table.

Any failures?

You know your successes. You've also got to know your failures and shortcomings, as well as those things you do not want in your future career. We'll analyze why certain things went wrong in the past and how to avoid the same pitfalls in the future. We'll identify what you do not want in your life.

Start with this simple, straightforward exercise.

Write the appropriate answers to the following:

1. What do you NOT want responsibility for?
   a._____
   b._____
   c._____
   d._____

2. What are the habits of others you find distasteful?
   a._____
   b._____
   c._____
   d._____

3. What types of people do you NOT enjoy working with?
   a._____
   b._____
   c._____
   d._____

4. Do you remember being reprimanded for performance in the past? What happened?
   a._____
   b._____
   c._____
   d._____

5. Look back at your life. Are there things you put off, failed at, gave half-hearted effort to or otherwise neglected? Would you change your approach to these things if you could go back in time? What would you do?

   a._____
   b._____
   c._____
   d._____

6. Look at Question #5 again. If you wrote that you'd do something differently if you could, could you do something about it now? Could you go back to school?

   Could you draw again, paint again, build again, etc..
   Do you want to do it now? What is it?

   a._____
   b._____
   c._____
   d._____

Here are some responses that reflect desires of people wanting to make changes in their lives:

"If I could, I'd have written those internal training manuals for the new computer system. I've provided research for others who've written manuals. I'm sure I could have done it."

"If I could, I'd have joined the project team that investigated new methods for streamlining our production line."

"If I could, I'd get out from behind my desk and organize a community recycling center."

"If I could, I'd join a building crew instead of this day to day grind behind the desk."

Change the "if I could" to "I will take the following steps so that I will become" and reap the rewards. Research what you want to do. Determine if you are qualified to do it. If you lack certain skills, do more research to determine how to get those skills. Then go out and get those skills!

If this whole process begins to overwhelm you, stop. Any frustrations will show in your efforts. Take a five minute walk. Or stretch for five minutes. Whatever you do, get away for a few minutes.

Now, when you've returned, do the following:

1. Identify why you are overwhelmed or frustrated. Maybe you can't think of any or all strengths. Perhaps you can't remember dates or names of people.
2. Ask your subconscious to do the work for you.
   Tell yourself your problem. Then go to sleep, take a nap, go to a movie, listen to soothing music, etc..

Whatever you do, develop the habit of keeping a small notebook and pen with you at all times. Next to the bed, in the car, in the kitchen, in your purse or coat pocket—wherever you are, when a solution to a problem comes to you, you must have the ability to write it down.

You may instruct your mind to begin a new way of thinking. It is imperative for you to get rid of any negative thoughts. Say goodbye to the following:

"I won't."
"I can't."
"I shouldn't."
"I'm not smart enough."
"I'll be embarrassed."
"I'm too fat."
"I'm too skinny."
"I'm too ugly, etc.."

You can come up with any number of excuses for not doing things in life. That's guaranteed. But, you can also list reason after reason for saying yes to doing those same things.

For self-improvement, ask yourself a dozen questions each day. Make sure the questions relate to bettering yourself. Do not ask negative questions. Then, listen for the answers.

Ask "How can I lose weight" as you go out the door to a movie.
Ask "What skills could I use in this new career" as you listen to the music of a favorite singer.
Ask "How can I earn more at my next job" as you continue your studies at the library.

Ask and listen.

The answers may be immediate. The answers may awaken you from a deep sleep. They make come to you as you're shampooing your hair. When the answers come, write them down.

You should ask questions to help every part of your job search. Questions and answers will help you in these many areas:

1. Finding out what you want to do in life.
2. Choosing to pursue some things while discarding others.
3. Deciding how to spend time at work and at home.
4. Learning new skills and values.
5. Bettering your income.
6. Meeting new people.
7. Increasing family happiness and security.

The list could go on and on.

Develop these qualities to meet your goals:

1. The ambition to succeed.
2. The motivation to do what it takes to succeed.
3. The energy to keep at it.
4. The determination not to let people or circumstances get you down.
5. The confidence to know you're doing the right thing.

6. The communication skills to let others help you along the way.

Develop and maintain these personal characteristics:

1. Honesty
2. Reliability
3. Dedication
4. Pride

Use and refine these skills:

1. The ability to analyze a problem.
2. The ability to research a problem.
3. The ability to listen.
4. The ability to solve a problem.
5. The ability to interact with others.
6. The ability to share with others.

Finally, prove to all concerned that:

1. You have the best skills to get a job done.
2. You have the best way for making or saving money.
3. You are one of the big reasons others achieve success.

People excel at those things they enjoy. Your work and your life go on at the same time. Enjoy both.

Research(By Industry, By Company)

Do not ignore this section.

Don't act like the many others who write their résumés, respond to ads and wait for their interviews. That approach may get you the interview and may get you the job. If that occurs, you can be certain it's because you've lowered your standards. You'll not give as much worth to yourself as you should. You'll allow the company to decide your future.

I wrote earlier that this period in time is part of the information society. No matter what your job is, information drives your success. Whatever industry, whatever company, you've got to understand their needs. You've got to prove you'll be one of their greatest assets. Whether you are a computer programmer, handle all incoming calls for a company, etc., information will lead you to success.

Think about our modified nursery rhyme that includes the banker(instead of a butcher), baker and candlestick maker. Assume we'll apply to each of them for a job. What do we want to show them? How will we benefit each of them? Let's look at each company and plan our attack.

Banker

We'll call our job seeker Judy. She has experience in accounting. Judy has worked for an accounting firm, a law firm and as a salesperson at a clothing store for two years while in college.

Through her research, Judy has made these important discoveries about the job prospect:

1. The downtown office has recently expanded into much larger quarters.
2. Company literature announced the appointment of a new legal director. The director spoke at length of the directions she wished to take the department and qualifications she looked for in staff support. Judy also requested and received the latest company prospectus.
3. Judy visited the reference section of the library for information about the company as a whole. She has learned that total employees have increased by about seven percent each year for the last five years. Sales and net revenue have increased at an even higher rate. Finally, various ratings firms give the company above-average ratings.

As you can see, Judy will have a great advantage over those who send in a résumé and wait for the interview. Those other people will tell the interviewer how great their skills are without relating any of them to the prospective employer.

Judy, on the other hand, will tell the interviewer the following:

1. "I have proven experience supervising the support unit of a law office as the department went through a total reorganization."
2. "Your company has grown steadily, at around 7% per year, over the past five years. I want to take part in that growth. I understand that with growth comes responsibility. My present employer is growing steadily and I've easily kept up with the resulting changes as they occurred."
3. "I'm confident that I have the qualifications needed to excel at this position. I have...".

Judy will then give her perception of their needs and how she will contribute to each of those needs.

This has been a general look at her investigation. Of course, with knowledge of the details about a company you'll be able to shine during the interview. Judy is well on her way to getting the job offer.

With our next two examples, you'll listen in on part of the interviews. We won't specifically cite the information found through research. Still, you'll realize what our job seekers have learned through their investigations:

Baker

1. "My name is Adam Smitts, Mr. Carvelli. I am very pleased to meet you."
2. "Thank you." (Adam has been asked to sit.)
3. "I'm very interested in your company. You have a reputation for growth by introducing products that the community asks for. I like that. I think satisfied customers are what makes your company prosper."
4. "I have skills that would contribute to your company, but no, I haven't worked in a bakery before."
5. "I excel at many things. I've done the books for a cleaning service. I've waited on tables and know the importance of appearance to the customer. I've supervised a team of six and assigned hours so that coverage matches the prime selling hours. I learn skills that will give me a well-rounded view of the service industry."
6. "I don't like employees eating in front of the customer. I think this gives the impression that we're servicing ourselves before them. The customer always has to come first. Especially in this business, where satisfied customers will come back every week for years and years.
7. "Let me check my appointment book. Yes, noon on Friday is fine. I really appreciate your further consideration. I know I will contribute great things to your company."

Candlestick Maker

1. "It is very nice to meet you, Mr. Brown. I've enjoyed our talks on the telephone and I'm glad we're now able to meet in person."

2. "To tell you the truth, Mr. Brown, I have never made a candle before. But my research tells me I could help you sell ten times as many candles as you do now."

3. "Well, I've noticed that most of your sales are made in the store. Over the last couple of months, I've seen how traffic seems to be level and that mailing packages to clients is not a regular occurrence.

4. "Mr. Brown, you make candles the same way they were made 200 years ago. This method is a great selling feature."

5. "I've got great computer skills. With your investment in me, I will open up whole new markets. At present, your clients are mostly from this area. I would develop advertising and mail order programs that would reach markets across the country.

6. "We would repackage your candles to attract enthusiasts of early American life. We could attract homeowners of many types, historians, preservation societies and their members, and more."

7. "The computer would keep records of all our contacts and enable us to sell to them year after year. The computer I own now would satisfy our needs for the first year. We could plan on a new computer purchase as we prove our growth."

8. "Yes, I'd love to meet your wife."

Be prepared. Do your research. The more you can tell a company about itself, the better your chances of keeping the interviewer interested in you.

You should know certain characteristics about an industry and about the companies to which you'll be applying for a job. Find answers to the following questions for each new industry and for every company, as applicable.

Industry Worksheet

1. How is this industry viewed in terms of future growth?

2. Is this industry considered stable or unstable?

3. What do government statistics show for projections of growth in number of employees over the next 5 years?

4. Does this industry support a large portion of your geographical area?

5. What services or products does this industry provide?

6. Can you determine the management style needed for companies in this industry to succeed?

Company Worksheet

1. Has this company grown over the past 5 years? By how much?

2. What rank does the company have in its industry? Has that rank gone up or down, or stayed the same, in the last 5 years?

3. When was this company established?

4. Does research suggest company stability or instability?

5. How many employees are there? Has there been growth in the number of employees? Does your research suggest growth will continue or occur in the future?

6. Is this company a leader in providing certain products or services? Do you have any strengths in those areas? How?

7. Does this company have the management style needed to prosper? Does management style match your own? You've read as many profiles about managers in the company as you could find. Do you approve of their style?

8. Are there other competitors in the area who could also benefit from your talents? (If so, fill out a Company Worksheet for them.) Would comparing companies during the interview help your cause?

9. Based upon your research, what different jobs in this company would you qualify for?

    a.
    b.
    c.

As you examine the marketplace, look at specific jobs to decide how they would benefit you. Yes, you'll show the company what you can do for them. You'll still have your own agenda. Decide if you can learn something from the job. Determine if opportunities for promotion are possible. Or, simply ask yourself if the job will add strength to your future résumé.

Do not limit your research. You may start by using a library. You may proceed by visiting employment agencies or the companies themselves(informational interviewing, discussed later). You should also get help from family and friends. Religious organizations and professional associations may help you a great deal. Your college may have special classes you can attend. Seminars and workshops may offer leads. However you approach the research, don't limit yourself.

Try to do as much research as possible before scheduling informational interviews. You'll gather and sort information. You'll come up with the best list of questions to ask. You'll also be better prepared for their questions.

Do you know that you'll build a list of references even before your first informational interview? Do you know what these references are?

They are the trade publications, company newsletters, community newspaper articles, investment ratings books, products themselves and so on. Mention these sources to your contacts. You'll impress them with the interest, honesty and enthusiasm you have towards their business.

Quick Tip

Here's an advance note concerning the informational interview. While you'll stress that a job offer is not what you are after at this time, some people find that job offers result from the process. An offer is very flattering. It may represent a great opportunity that should be accepted. Or, the offer may not be in your best interest. If you've done your research fully, you'll know the difference.

If an offer is made, follow these procedures:

1. Decide if you're actually prepared to accept. Will the job make you happy, both personally and in terms of career success(money, promotions, adding skills, etc..)?

2. Do you have enough knowledge to compare this offer with what future offers will comprise(are you sure the money offered will be the best that's possible)?

3. Does your 'gut feeling' tell you to take the job? (Remember, learn to have 'gut feelings' to promote growth. Do not let negative thoughts force you to settle for less.)

4. As with cover letters, résumés and job interviews (all discussed in later chapters), have you discussed salary history to your disadvantage?

Etiquette

During the interview, share your observations about the industry. Don't be directly critical ("your company has to get its head out of the sand"), but do show you've researched a perceived problem. For instance, "Sales have become flat on this product. Do you see changing product design or marketing focus as a means to generate growth?".

When you've gathered all your research materials you'll need to review all you've learned. Good and bad. The easiest way to analyze what has transpired is to fill out the following chart. Take your time and weigh your analysis carefully.

Recap of Research	Yes/No/Comments
1. Do they have problems I can solve?	
2. Did I like the person I met related to this field?	
3. Does the company seem to be a good one?	
4. Is there work there that I could do?	
5. Could I learn new skills there?	
6. Would my contributions be noticed?	
7. Would I like the people and environment?	
8. Are there advancement opportunities?	
9. Based upon the above, should I pursue this industry and/or company?	

For further detail on the particular company you've researched, write yourself a summary of qualifications based on what they need and what you can do. Again, you'll fill out a chart. Here is an example:

What They Need	What I Can Do
1. Someone to type 50 wpm	1. I can type 70 wpm.
2. Someone self-reliant	2. I can work without direct supervision.
3. A team player	3. I'm on time, committed to deadlines and support the needs of the group.

4. Someone knowing shorthand	4.I don't know shorthand, but I can use a computer to input memos the boss recites into a tape recorder. This would allow me to work while the stenographer would be taking notes.
5. Someone not young and irresponsible	5. I'm young and very responsible. Qualifications will prove that.

Now it's your turn:

What They Need	**What I Can Do**
1.	1.
2.	2.
3.	3.
4.	4.
5.	5.

As you fill these charts out, you'll begin to notice similar needs throughout a particular industry or job level. You'll determine where companies need to add strength. Through your early analysis you'll build a foundation that will be beneficial to you during the actual job interview process.

The recap of the research process serves yet another purpose. By analyzing a broad segment of an industry or group of companies, you'll be able to narrow down your job search. You may decide on one or two companies where you really want to work. At that time, all out effort may be applied solely to those companies.

Quick Tip

Sometimes, a job offer may come totally unexpectedly.

You may ask, "I said I wasn't expecting a job offer. Plus, they also told me they weren't hiring, so how is it possible for me to choose whether the company is right for me?" In response, we can only remind you that people retire, get fired, relocate, get promoted, take extended leave, accept positions at other companies and so on. Opportunities will always arise.

Or, you may quickly realize working with a certain person or firm would fulfill many of your dreams.

Here is an approach to use if you want to try for an unspecified position after a bit of successful research. Let's assume you were impressed by the company and the people you met. You know you could use all your talents and learn new skills. You'd be contributing to the company and to yourself.

Read the following letter and decide if a similar approach would benefit you:

Dear Mrs. Kimball:

Since we last met, I have been thinking a great deal about the issues facing your company. I've continued my research of your company and the industry and I am very excited by what I've learned. I'm sure that I could make significant contributions to the company in a number of ways.

You face a challenging market. I have prepared a list of these challenges, together with the ways my qualifications would benefit each.

<u>**Challenges**</u>
Marketing a new product

<u>**My Qualifications**</u>
Marketed Z Brand to national market, penetrating opposition sales. Claimed 8% of market nationally, 15% in the Northeast sector.

<u>**Challenges**</u>
Overseeing 10 sales offices

<u>**My Qualifications**</u>
Oversaw 12 sales offices. Created 30% of sales for company. Expanded to new territories. Grew from 9 to 12 territories in one year. Increased net return for company. Garnered a profit higher than start–up costs in first year of operations.

I would like to speak with you briefly. Your feedback would be most appreciated. I will call you on (day), (date) at (time). You are welcome to call me at any time.

I very much look forward to speaking with you soon.

Sincerely,

(Your Name)

Save all your notes and correspondences. Set up a filing system to store this material. Treat your research as you would a diary. The information is personal and confidential and is your property only. At some point you will again review these notes from the past and use them to develop your future.

Material that is not relevant today may become extremely valuable tomorrow. You may change job locations. You may change the focus of your career. Your research will supply a good foundation for subsequent efforts.

The Informational Interview

One of the most important aspects of the informational interview is timing. You'll want to have enough time to find out what you need, but you must also respect the actual time given to you. It may seem odd, but you should always plan your session based on the proper time for you to leave it.

First, this is important because you've already agreed to a set period of time. Second, you want to base your analysis on a productive session that gets you to the next stage of your job search. Third, you'll want to impress the contact with the value you give their time. And last, you'll show that you are committed to what you say.

Why do you want to conduct an informational interview?

1. To gain information on an industry.
2. To gain information on a company.
3. To gain advice on job prospects in an industry, qualifications needed to excel, growth prospects, changes expected, salary ranges, etc..
4. To gain referrals for further research.

Did you notice each of the four items listed above begin with 'to gain'? You can only gain positive results from the informational interview. The experience will benefit you, even if it didn't seem to work out.

Let's say you're going to an interview. The industry is very appealing to you. Now, fast forward 20 minutes. Your contact at the interview was grumpy. The boss interrupted your session to belittle your contact. His office and those around him were cigarette smoke-filled, with the occasional scent of cigars wafting through the air. You hate smoking. By the way, you've not yet seen anybody smile.

How fortunate for you to have gained so much! You still believe in your research. Now you can add insight to what environment you don't want to participate in. You probably found many things in that office you could do better. Plus, you can weigh this knowledge against your interviews with other companies in the same industry.

Two methods of communication will serve you well in getting informational interviews. They are writing letters and making telephone calls.

Letters and telephone calls are important for several reasons, such as:

1. Introducing yourself to new contacts.
2. Using contact names as referrals on your letters and telephone calls.
3. Thanking a contact for their information.
4. Asking for clarification on earlier material provided.
5. Pursuing additional meetings.
6. Suggesting your availability.
7. Reminding the interviewer of your name and abilities.

A well written letter and a polite telephone manner will give you great advantages over the competition. As with everything else in the job search, a poor presentation, whether written or oral, will certainly hurt you. Perhaps you'll still get the information or the job, but you may have to work harder for it.

To avoid common mistakes, I've highlighted some of the primary rules for writing effective letters. Where appropriate, use these same rules as a guideline for your telephone conversations. They are:

1. Keep the letter to one page only. For telephone conversations, don't ask for or expect more than 5 minutes of time.

2. Spell everything correctly. If you aren't sure of the contacts full name or title, call the secretary, look at published information, etc.. You might even call the contact and ask for correct information so that you can send them a 'package'. You do not have to identify yourself at that moment. People receive packages everyday and are more than happy to see that it reaches them in proper fashion.

3. Show some connection to the contact. If you got their name through referral, by all means include the name of the referral. If not, make an effort to show admiration for the contact, their company or their products. Suggest that you share a similar background. However you do it, your first connection to the reader should create a strong first impression.

4. Explain the purpose of your letter. Tell them you are researching the industry. Say that you have skills that could contribute, but that you want to be sure you'll contribute as best as possible. Suggest that the contact could direct you further. Maybe you'd want them to suggest types of further education or skills that would better prepare you for your job search.

5. Make the contact feel at ease. State that you are not pressing them for a job. Instead, stress that you are exploring the opportunities that exist in the marketplace. Praise them and tell them their knowledge and experience will be of great assistance to you.

6. Close the letter by saying what next steps you'll take. Do not give them any work to do. You tell them when you'll follow through with a telephone call, noting the day, date and time.

7. Thank them sincerely and tell them you look forward to speaking with them and seeing them in the near future.

A Special Note

It is imperative that you stick to the day, date and time specified. A half hour delay, or calling the next day will seriously reduce your chances of meeting your contact.

For Telephone Callers

Be prepared. Using a telephone may seem the quickest way to get what you want. Still, using a telephone does not remove any of the responsibilities you have. In fact, your skills must be at their best because you'll be able to succeed or fail, according to the contact, within 30 seconds. To get the interview, observe the following:

1. Be polite and use clear language.
2. Open the conversation with a connection.
3. Explain your purpose.
4. Ask for the meeting.
5. Close the conversation with sincere appreciation.

And always have the following at hand when calling:

1. Paper
2. Pen
3. Calculator, if necessary
4. Organized notes
5. Good questions to ask

Conducting informational interviews will not simply involve companies where you want to work. Informational interviews can and should be conducted wherever you can get information. Information that will a help better your chances for a great job.

Different approaches for different sources should be used. All sources should receive the highest degree of personalization possible. Letters should be individually written, then typed or put into your word processor. Certain considerations will be given to particular audiences.

As a guideline, consider the samples represented on the next pages. Each contains an overview statement before the actual sample is given. The letters cover the large corporate business, recruiters, agencies(such as temporary assignments or permanent placement), professional organizations, civic organizations, religious affiliations and previous professional associates.

Large Corporate Business

Overview: Whether or not you think the large corporate office is a wasteful bureaucracy with unlimited free time, or on the cutting edge of new technologies, treat your contact with a respect for their valued time. Before you write to them or call them, find out if the company has a corporate library. If so, go there and learn as much as you can about the company(products, employees, etc.). The corporate library may be for employees only, but you'll figure a way to use the library as a resource.

Sample:

Salutation:

Your name was given to me by Peter Standahl, Vice President of Perkins-Waning & Gronz Company. He spoke very highly of your accomplishments and felt you could be very helpful to me.

You have broad experience in the systems development field. At this time, I am looking into various areas related to this industry. I have worked for over nine years at Hanson Corporation in the product development division. I am most interested in your suggestions regarding the potential opportunities ahead for this industry.

Be assured that I am not looking for a position from you. Rather, I would appreciate your advice on how my background can best serve the industry.

I will call you next week to set up a mutually convenient meeting.

Sincerely,

Your Name

Recruiter or Headhunter

Overview: Writing to a recruiter or headhunter is very different than writing to a corporation. In this instance, you'll want the recruiter to work for you. Still, you've got to sell yourself to them in order to get on their roster of talented people.

Sample:

Your Address

Date

Their Name
Title
Full Address

Salutation:

After more than twelve years as Senior Marketing Analyst at Able Bank, I am looking for a new position where I can contribute more fully to the industry.

As shown on my attached résumé, my record of opening new markets is substantial. I've been able to build teams from scratch, then develop a leading position in product share.

If you consider my skills appropriate for one of your clients, I would like to meet with you for further discussion.

I will call you next week to set up a meeting.

Sincerely,

Your Name

Agency (Temporary or Permanent Placement)

Overview: Temporary work assignments can lead to great job offers. If you are unsure of where you would fit best, temporary assignments will help you with self-definition. Plus, you may learn new skills which open up other opportunities. Be prepared to work immediately. Also, allow yourself to refuse assignments not in your best interests. Finally, a temporary assignment that could turn into a permanent job may or may not be best for you. Use all the research and analysis skills you'll develop throughout this book to make the right choices for a career.

Sample:

Salutation:

After more than three years in desktop publishing, I am looking for new opportunities that will give me broader experience in the field.

Your company has a reputation for placing highly skilled workers in demanding and exciting positions. As the attached résumé shows, I am fully qualified to meet those demands presented by your clients.

I am willing to explore many areas of the fields you may offer. I would like to meet with you to discuss the ways I would benefit you and your clients.

I will call you next week to set up an appointment.

Sincerely,

Your Name

Professional Organizations and Associations

Overview: Most industries have associations which support the aims of the workers and companies they represent. They can be a tremendous help in leading you in the right and best direction. Associations are made up of those people most proud of their professions and most willing to help you.

Sample:

Your Address

Date

Their Name
Title
Full Address

Salutation:

Your association is most impressive. I've seen that the best companies in the plastics industry are members and consider you a valuable resource.

I am a plastics engineer with four years experience in the field. As my attached résumé shows, I've consulted on various assignments throughout the Northeast.

At this time, I would like to explore other opportunities in the field. The time and assistance you provide to association members and other individuals is invaluable. I would like you to help me set my job campaign on the right course. I know your insights will benefit my search.

I will call you next week to set up a meeting.

Sincerely,

Your Name

Civic Organizations

Overview: Similar to the professional associations, the civic organizations provide a wealth of information. Especially valuable are the ways a civic group can help someone who has recently settled in the area.

Sample:

> Your Address
>
> Date

Their Name
Title
Full Address

Salutation:

I have recently moved to this area. My decision to move here was based on the opportunities for education, involvement with the many arts groups and growth in high-tech employment.

Civic leaders of your sister city, San Francisco, suggested my skills could be utilized more fully here. As my attached résumé shows, my experience will provide a valuable contribution to the community.

I would like to meet with you to explore ways I could contribute.

I will call you next week to set up a mutually convenient meeting.

> Sincerely,
>
> Your Name

Religious Affiliation

Overview: Your minister, rabbi or other contact has broad-based connections to the community. While they supply much needed spiritual nourishment, they may also provide the perfect job lead. Your contact may know you well enough to suggest which companies your skills and personality would fit in best with. And if you've been recently laid-off or fired, they'll help you. This is one group of people that will not want to see you suffer.

Sample:

Salutation:

I have been a member of your congregation for two years. I've enjoyed your services and have found inspiration in much of what you've said.

I am exploring the possibility of changing career direction. I've been an administrative assistant for a local advertising agency for three years. At present, I'm considering other aspects of the publishing industry as well as direct marketing.

I would appreciate your suggestions as to how I could approach this change. You would provide valuable insights into opportunities that exist in our community.

I look forward to speaking with you after this Sunday's service.

Sincerely,

Your Name

Previous Professional Associates

Overview: Just as you'll be extremely careful choosing your references, be careful which former professional associates you ask for help. Former associates can be a valuable resource. They might also hurt your chances for success. Know their intentions. Make sure your interests are their primary concern.

Sample:

Your Address

Date

Their Name
Title
Full Address

Salutation:

During the last 8 weeks, I've been considering my contributions to our industry. You were very helpful when we worked on special projects together. I could really use your help as I now consider my future.

I've put together a summary of qualifications that I'd like you to review. I'm looking to address my areas of strengths and weaknesses. Your assessment of my job skills would contribute a great deal to my analysis.

I'll call you on Thursday to hear what you think. I'd be glad to come in for a brief meeting at any mutually convenient time.

I look forward to speaking with you.

Sincerely,

Your Name

You can develop a great many contacts if you try. Do you respect your neighbor? How about your banker? Were you recently visiting your doctor or dentist? What about your golfing buddies or the bowling team? What about that club you belong to that has 50 members? When you travelled to that conference last year, didn't you exchange business cards with people from all over the country?

Use as many contacts as necessary to build your future.

Those Valuable Assistants

In every profession, assistants support busy people at every level. Many times, those same assistants plan the activities of the day for their bosses. An assistant can be your greatest resource. Some bosses depend on their assistant more than they depend on family or friends.

Treat every assistant with respect. Ask for their help. Be polite. Know their name and use it. Ask them to spell their name, if needed, and show them you are writing it down. Thank them at every opportunity. Show your appreciation with a sincere smile. Above all, say thank you and mean it.

Writing Your Job Objective

Have you ever worked in advertising? If you have, you know that if the headline doesn't grab the audience the audience is lost. Your job objective will have the same function. The job objective must convey the kind of job you want. At the same time, it will be general enough not to limit some important prospects. In every case, you'll show how you use your best strengths to achieve results.

You have a list of strengths. You've known what makes you happy and proud. You are aware of your great contributions to previous employers. With these strengths in mind, your job objective statement will be written. The job objective has three purposes:

1. To identify what you want to do in your next job.

2. To show the qualities you have to succeed in the position.

3. To deliver on results the company will get by hiring you.

The first purpose is important to understand. Notice the words 'to do' are written, not 'to be'. There is an important difference.

We'll prove the difference with an example. If you're telling a prospective employer what you are 'to be', you might say "I am a programmer in COBOL". You've been a programmer in COBOL before and you want to be so again.

Now, let's tell the prospective employer what you'll do. "I'll do programming that will help the organization run more efficiently."

Do you see what the employer may think of the two contenders for the job. If not, listen to the job objectives with a negative reaction from the employer. Simply write "We don't need" before the main part of the job objective. For example:

1. "We don't need a programmer in COBOL."

2. "We don't need programming that will help the organization run more efficiently."

The employer could very well respond as such in the first example if they needed someone with different programming language skills. Yet, an employer would never say that they didn't need the company to run more efficiently.

If the employer screens the résumés out based on whether the person can program in something other than COBOL, here's what will happen.

1. The first résumé will be immediately discarded.

2. With the second, the employer will likely read through the résumé to determine what the prospect can do for the company.

To give yourself a very particular job title or objective is to limit yourself in the marketplace. Do not expect the employer to infer anything simply because you have a certain title. Remember that a title is not a qualification.

Every employer knows jobs have titles. They also know you may identify with a title. More importantly, though, they'll want to know what you'll do for them. You must show them what you know, what you'll do and how you'll do more. You'll show them how you'll learn new skills. You'll demonstrate how you will adapt to your new environment. Contributing and getting results, both on your own and as part of a team, will be primary skills you'll display. Make or save them money and you'll get the job.

Are you what you were 5 or 10 years ago? Probably not. Likewise, understand that whatever you'll be doing in your job today will not be exactly the same 1, 3 or 5 years from now. You've got to remind the employer of these realities through action and example.

Here are two job objectives. You'll see the writing process at work. After reviewing the examples, use the same process to write your own job objective.

Example Number One

1. *What do you want to do in your next job?*

   I want to manage accounts at a chemical manufacturing company.

2. *What basic qualities do you have to succeed in this job, from the perspective of the employer?*

   I've handled some of the biggest accounts at my last company. Teams are important to success and I've been a team leader on three important product launchings.

3. *What results will the company get by hiring you?*

   Well, my clients contributed as much as 30% to the company profits each year.

Now, combine the answers to the 3 questions into one powerful job objective statement.

Job Objective

- Specializing as a senior manufacturing account manager for large, high–priority accounts contributing substantial bottom–line profits.

Example Number Two

1. *What do you want to do in your next job?*

   I think I'd like to work in a bank as an administrative assistant in the Real Estate division.

2. *What basic qualities do you have to succeed in this job, from the perspective of the employer?*

   I can use all office equipment, including computers and various software packages. I've been an assistant before and I've even helped senior managers on special projects.

3. *What results will the company get by hiring you?*

   I know what I'm doing. The company doesn't have to spend alot of time helping me learn how to use new equipment. I can also work overtime and I'll take home special projects to work on, if necessary.

Job Objective

- Supporting administrative teams, with proven dedication to office operations and management–directed special projects.

It's time for you to write your own job objective. First, answer the three questions:

1. What do you want to do in your next job?

2. What basic qualities do you have to succeed in this job, from the perspective of the employer?

3. What results will the company get by hiring you?

<u>Job Objective</u>

•

Stated correctly, you'll highlight your interests, your abilities and the contributions you'll make to the company.

Your Summary of Qualifications

At the beginning of the last chapter you were asked if you ever worked in advertising. Even if you said no, you may have written advertising copy at some point in the past.

Have you ever placed an ad to sell something you owned? Perhaps an old stereo, an appliance, a coveted antique, etc.? If so, you probably gave a brief description of what the item was, facts or information that would make that item interesting to potential buyers. At the very least, depending on how attractive the offer, a number of buyers would get in touch with you for more information. Some would even make an offer. And one lucky buyer would get the prize!

To get a job offer you also must sell a product. You! A summary of qualifications is similar to the sub–heading of an advertisement. You'll tell the reader who you are and qualities about yourself that would interest them. And what about your price? Well, the qualities you promote will imply your worth.

The advertisement reader is grabbed in three steps. First, you'll grab them with the headline, your job objective. Next, you'll entice them with more benefits with any sub–headings, your summary of qualifications. Finally, you'll clinch the deal with the meat of the text, your experience, education and so on.

Don't become confused between the meaning of the job objective versus the summary of qualifications. Both do not contain the same information. The job objective gives the reader what they need. The summary of qualifications "qualifies" that need with benefits.

Let's look at two examples. One is a can opener. The other is a person.

Can Opener

Job Objective

- Specializing in kitchen support to 5–star restaurant.

Summary of Qualifications

- Long–lasting, durable machine supporting the most demanding usage. Long cord, no rusting and sharp cutter, combined with battery attachment for power outages offer highest standards in industry.

Person

Job Objective

- Specializing in systems analysis for critical management–defined functions.

Summary of Qualifications

- Using in–depth knowledge of four programming languages and micro environments to support special projects for all levels of management.

Not only should the second step be supported by the first, the second step should entice the reader to move on to the third. The third, of course, being the details of experience.

Think about our person example. If our systems analyst had listed the four languages in the job objective and our reader needed one different from the four, her chances of getting the job would be lessened. Similarly, identify the languages in the summary of qualifications and the reader may not reach the details.

Look at what has happened instead:

1. We've said we can do critical systems work.

2. We've shown management agrees and uses our many talents.

3. We've invited the reader to continue on and benefit from our proven abilities.

Your Summary of Qualifications

In the preceding chapter you wrote your job objective. Write it again here:

_____

_____

Does the job objective still appear attractive. Is it clear to the general reader? Is it brief? Have you avoided language that might limit your possibilities?

If you are satisfied with your job objective, we'll proceed to your own summary of qualifications.

Can you back up what you've written as your job objective? How? If you want to be President and CEO, do you have all the most important skills a President and CEO has? What are those qualifications? Once you know what you want, you'll support your desire with summarized qualifications.

Review your ten power statements from Chapter 3, 'Focusing on Strengths'. Select the five statements that best combine your strengths and interests. (If you are the best orator around yet hate public speaking, leave it off this section.)

Now, rewrite your five best power statements. You may write them as before or refine them further.

Five Power Statements

-

-

-

-

-

Now, highlight a single word or phrase from each that summarizes each strength.

Can you combine these highlighted words and phrases into one cohesive summary of qualifications? Does this summary support the job objective while at the same time entice the reader to move on? If not, this example may help you:

<u>Five Power Statements</u>

- Converted 25 processes maintained on subsystems, p.c.'s and manual forms to a new system.

- Conducted in–depth training classes on new hardware and software, training 30 staff members from all levels of management.

- Verified that 30 staff members are able to balance cash and assets on the system.

- Initiated research project that uncovered lost fees. Recovered over $40,000 in three months.

- Supervised five support staff who processed all documents for 15 officers.

Job Objective

- Specializing in systems conversions, training and quality assurance

Summary of Qualifications

- Uncovering underreported income based on profit oriented project analysis. Training all levels of staff to properly utilize systems, using expertise to bridge management needs with technical expertise to arrive at project resolutions.

The best way to write your summary of qualifications is to write it, revise it and write it again. Write it over and over again until it is clear and impressive. You should not use any language that may limit potential offers. When you cannot change a single word or phrase you will have arrived at the most satisfying result.

Yet again, it's your turn. Write the highlighted words and phrases from your power statements:

-
-
-
-
-

Summarize. Build one or two strong sentences. Don't repeat your job objective or your power statements. Instead, entice the reader. Invite the reader to explore the details. Keep working at it until you've got what you want.

Your Summary of Qualifications

●

That's great! You should be pleased at how well your résumé is progressing. In the next chapter we'll move on to the details.

Your Work Experience

You are like everyone else in one important way. You bring skills to your job and to your life each day. There are more skills you'll learn throughout your life. Some skills will become less important as others replace them. Through it all, there are incredible talents you have that play an important role in your personal and professional life.

Skills translate into what your paycheck is now and what that paycheck will become in the future. 'Now' could be tomorrow when you accept a job offer. 'The future' might be three months later when you're asked to bring other skills to the company. What you will become is determined by the skills you offer the company.

Think about what you can offer. How would the company react to you if you said the following:

"I am very interested in the position. I've developed skills that qualify me for the position. More importantly, and as proven with my past record, I can change as a job changes. New technology, new management philosophies and new work partners are all taken in stride. I'll grow however I can to help the company grow."

Assume two people are equally qualified. If one of them makes the above statement, whom would you hire? Your qualifications are your past. The new employer was not part of your past. Say this aloud three times:

"The employer wants me for what I'll become."
"The employer wants me for what I'll become."
"The employer wants me for what I'll become."

You are great now. Prove that you'll add to that greatness.

Now you've got to show your past as it will benefit the future. The employer only cares about what you can do for them. You know that, but also realize a hidden agenda of your own. Your hidden agenda is determining what the employer can do for you!

Just as jobs change, you want to be satisfied that those changes will be to your benefit. If you bring 5 strong skills to a new position and through job changes you now utilize only 3 of them, you are in trouble. Continue to utilize only 3 skills and you'll soon be out of the running for promotion. Even worse, doing less may give the company reason to do without you.

Of course, changes in technology and management philosophies can replace your 5 skills with 5 or more new ones. You must show your employer you are always doing more, not less.

Your past will get you to the future. With these points made, some may have questions about their own perceived inadequacies. We'll ask a few questions and answer them.

1. "I don't have a great job now, so what can I expect?"

You can expect to achieve whatever you want as long as you build a foundation to get it. Read about the CEOs of major corporations across America. Some have vast educational experience. Some have college degrees, high school degrees or no degrees of any kind, including high school. But they planned every step of their future. Make your own plans. When you reach a goal, set a new goal. Never rest on an achievement. Know that everyone has a past. No matter what level of executive, everyone was something before what they are at present. Use your skills to develop your future.

2. "I've been working for myself, so how can I prove how valuable I'd be to someone else?"

First, congratulations! Working for yourself takes determination and a high degree of confidence in yourself. To successfully reenter the job marketplace, complete each section of this book. You'll find that skills you used to support yourself before will easily support another company. (Even if you didn't succeed at your own business, your attempt itself was a learning experience. Don't discount anything you learn, even if the learning came from a negative experience.)

3. "I've never gone to college. What's out there for me?"

Everything. Remember the fundamental rule of the job search. Show what you can do for someone else. Solve their problems. If you can prove you'll be a benefit to them, you'll go far. Take as an example Samuel Clemens. He didn't graduate from high school. Still, he used his skills to *become* Mark Twain, one of the greatest American writers.

4. "I just graduated from college with a 2.5 average. How am I going to land a great job?"

You also deserve congratulations. Did college teach you new skills? Did you graduate through your own efforts? Be proud of your efforts, not a statistical average. With regard to the job market, who says you have to advertise your grade average? The graduate with a 4.0 may have had no social life and thus no social skills, no associations with sports or the school newspaper, etc.. What's your story? Did you participate in sports? Were you working while attending school? Were you a lab or research assistant? Your 2.5 does nothing for the company. Your skills do.

5. "I've been doing the exact same job for 20 years. What is my future?"

What do you want it to be? Are you still doing the same job as you were 20 years ago? Haven't you kept up with any of the new technologies? (In the last 20 years, we've had the introduction of the electric typewriter, high–speed copying equipment, the fax machine, personal computers and the software for them, etc..) Did you volunteer for any special projects over the years? When you've completed all the exercises in this book, you'll have the tools to define your future. A great future.

6. "I haven't worked at all for ten years. How can I show someone that I'm worth hiring?"

What have you been doing for the ten years? Were you raising a family, going to school, writing a book, etc.? Did you work before this ten year period? In every circumstance, define your accomplishments. If you've raised a family and never worked at all, analyze those skills you do have. Organizing schedules. Budgeting. Accounting skills(for the little league). You do have skills, but only you can define them. Complete the exercises and you'll be able to show your worth to every employer. And remember, every single person, no matter how qualified, will face rejections. You will too, but that doesn't lessen your worth.

7. "I am quite literally afraid of the world. I've got to get another job but am frightened by the whole process. What should I do?

In what ways are your frightened? Do you mean that you don't like working in a large office? If so, how about working in an office with only 3 people? Or, how about telecommuting? Could you put a computer in your home and get your work assignments through the mail or modem? Could you work at night and avoid most of the work force? If you don't want to participate with other groups, slant your research towards your interests. Research will identify what is best for you. Once defined, you can go after your ideal job.

8. "I'm disabled. Who is going to hire me?

First, determine how you are 'abled'. What can you do for them? You'll be valued according to how you can benefit your associates, your boss and your company. Define your skills. Research companies to determine if they fulfill any requirements needed by you because of your disability. If they meet your requirements, remove your disability from their eyes and yours. Sell your skills. Sell how great you are.

9. *"I'm too old, young, fat, skinny, ugly or pretty? What should I do?"*

Take a look around. Better yet, stand outside the entrance to a large company when business hours start. Does everyone walking through the door fit an ideal image that you are not part of? Of course not. They sold their skills and their physical appearance. So should you. Keeping well–groomed, including a nice haircut and clean, filed fingernails, flattering yourself with fine clothing, good shoes and so on will enhance your appearance considerably. Whatever concern you have regarding your appearance, use the research skills outlined in this book to learn how to improve your self-image.

10. *"I'm African–American, Hispanic, Chinese, Lebanese, Portuguese, etc.. How am I going to deal with the attitudes out there?"*

First, realize that some sort of bias exists for every living person on this planet. Somewhere, for whatever reason, every person will be disliked. If you deal with the attitudes inside yourself, you'll have no problems that can't be overcome. Again, research, research and more research is the key. As long as you use the fabulous qualities of your ethnic background, combined with your skills, to show how you'll benefit the company you will succeed.

I've answered ten basic sets of questions. There are more answers, just as there are more questions. You have to understand that nothing in life is 100% guaranteed. It is your strengths that will get you through life.

The ten sets of questions may be attitudes others have towards you. More importantly, you may also have these attitudes about yourself. Two important points should be remembered:

1. Some people will always find fault with you.

Some people, and companies, will not hire you for a job you're qualified for. Your sex may be X, your color may be Y and your weight may be Z. And so on. Yes, this is immoral and illegal, yet it does happen. You must think of this as a tremendous loss for the company, not for you.

Assume you are hired knowing or sensing their reservations about you. How is your personal dignity affected while you're disproving their poor judgement about your character? Know that a company with these underlying attitudes and principles will eventually fail. Why be part of it?

2. You may find fault with yourself.

It is time to be very blunt. Take a deep breath or splash some cold water on your face before reading the next paragraph if you like. Here we go:

If you have and keep these attitudes about yourself, you will have less in life. Your self-esteem will be less. So too, you'll have less money and less possessions. You'll settle for a lesser home. You'll be less active in friendships, hobbies and outdoor activities. You'll choose to have less than the best health. Finally, you'll grow less than others in your career.

Do you need another deep breath?

Look at someone who seems to have everything and has worked for none of it. A great house, great possessions and travelling the world over. Through their fortune (or misfortune), they've only had to put their hand out to receive these things. Have they accomplished anything? Yes! They have put their hand out.

Unfortunately, they haven't learned any skills except that one. If someone else stops filling their hand, they'll be lost.

You too have got to put your hand out. Only remember that you are not putting out your hand for the end results(the money, etc.), you are putting your hand out for the skills, abilities and opportunities that are on offer.

Do you realize that reading this book means you have taken a step forward to better yourself? Keep that same attitude in everything you do in life. With that attitude every kind of success will come your way.

The Big Quiz

Starting with the present, can you move backwards through time to the age of 13 and identify where you were at all times. Can you identify the jobs you've held, the years you held them and the titles for each? Can you remember which skills you used at each job? You may find this easy to do. If so, can you do the same for your 'life values'?

With a substantial career and life history, you may not remember if you were in Boston or New York in the fall of 1973. Similarly, if you belonged to the PTA when your child was in school we have three questions for you. Which child? What school? What year(s)?

Knowing these details will prove important to your résumé writing and in your interviewing. Take your time filling out the next exercise. Simply answer the questions as fully and accurately as possible.

Experience Chart   Your Answers

1. What is the name of the company you work for now?
   •
   Where is your job? (City, State)
   •
   What is your title?
   •
   Through research, what else could you call yourself?
   •
   What year, year only, did you begin this job?
   •

1A. If you are not working now, what would you say you do?
   •

   Where do you do this? (City, State)
   •

   Through research, what title could you call yourself?
   •

   What year or years have you been doing this?
   •

2. What title did you have before the one above?
   •

   What else could you call yourself?
   •

   Was this job for the same company?
   •

   If not, what company was it?
   •

   Where was this job? (City, State)
   •

   What year or years did you have this job?
   •

3. What title did you have before the one above?
   •

   What else could you call yourself?
   •

   Was this job for the same company?
   •

   If not, what company was it?
   •

   Where was this job? (City, State)
   •

   What year or years did you have this job?
   •

4. What title did you have before the one above?
   •

   What else could you call yourself?
   •

   Was this job for the same company?
   •

If not, what company was it?
•

Where was this job? (City, State)
•

What year or years did you have this job?
•

5. What title did you have before the one above?
   •

   What else could you call yourself?
   •

   Was this job for the same company?
   •

   If not, what company was it?
   •

   Where was this job? (City, State)
   •

   What year or years did you have this job?
   •

6. What title did you have before the one above?
   •

   What else could you call yourself?
   •

   Was this job for the same company?
   •

   If not, what company was it?
   •

   Where was this job? (City, State)
   •

   What year or years did you have this job?
   •

7. What title did you have before the one above?
   •

   What else could you call yourself?
   •

   Was this job for the same company?
   •

   If not, what company was it?
   •

Where was this job? (City, State)
-

What year or years did you have this job?
-

8. What title did you have before the one above?
   -

   What else could you call yourself?
   -

   Was this job for the same company?
   -

   If not, what company was it?
   -

   Where was this job? (City, State)
   -

   What year or years did you have this job?
   -

9. Do you belong to any professional associations?
   What is the name of the organization?
   -

   Where do you meet?
   -

   Do you have a specific job there? Is there a title?
   -

   What year or years have you been involved?
   -

10. Do you belong to any other associations or organizations?
    What is the name of the organization?
    -

    Where do you meet?
    -

    Do you have a specific job there? Is there a title?
    -

    What year or years have you been involved?
    -

11. Many people have hobbies. Do you?
    What is the hobby?
    -

Where do you do this?
-

Is this hobby carried out as part of a group?
-

Do you have a specific role? Do you have a title?
-

What year or years have you been involved?
-

12. If you went to college, which college?
-

What major(s) did you have?
-

What degree(s) do you have?
-

What year did you graduate?
-

If you didn't graduate, what year(s) did you attend?
-

Continue in the same manner all the way back through your work and life careers and education. You may have one item or twenty. It does not matter as long as you identify them. Some things, such as education, special technical courses, memberships in professional associations, or the pursuit of hobbies are interspersed throughout our lives. If so, give them their own identity. Overlap years if necessary but let them stand on their own.

Finish this exercise on a blank sheet of paper if necessary. Do not discount any of your history.

What work you've done! Identifying your past takes effort and an attention to detail. (Two qualities much in demand in the work place.) After you've rested for a few minutes, do the next exercise. Treat it as a game. Simply circle each word or phrase that applies to you. Be honest but at the same time don't undercut your abilities.

Circle as appropriate:

ORGANIZED	WORK STUDY	FLEXIBLE
PROVEN LEADER	STRATEGIST	DESIGNER
DISCIPLINED	WRITER	ADVISOR
HISTORY BUFF	SHOPPER	RESULTS–ORIENTED
TEACHER	VOLUNTEER	DETAILED
TRUSTWORTHY	CAMPAIGNER	PILOT
LECTURER	RESEARCHER	SOLDIER
GARDENER	REPAIRMAN	CABINET–MAKER
PAINTER	SPORTSMAN	ACTIVIST
RESTORER	GAMESMAN	SINGER
COMMUNICATOR	COORDINATOR	DANCER
IMAGINATIVE	QUILTMAKER	HONEST
BUILDER	INVESTIGATOR	TEAM
COLLECTOR	PERSUASIVE	PLAYER
ASSEMBLER	NEGOTIATOR	MANAGER
CONTROLLER	DRESSMAKER	ANALYST
AVID READER	TRAVELLER	ACTOR

YOUR CHOICE: _____

YOUR CHOICE: _____

The best part of this exercise is that you win just by playing! You'll win because you may want to incorporate some of those talents into your résumé.

Did you circle the word 'researcher'? If not, I'll give you another chance. I'll list it again. With full intentions of making research one of your abilities, circle the word.

RESEARCHER

Composing Your Résumé

"We live in an information society." You have heard that often enough, haven't you? What does it mean to you? You should understand that an information society rests on inequality. Most often, these inequalities are handled in a multi-level, cooperative process.

Let's look at an example.

I have a speech to make. The speech is composed of four parts. I am an expert in one part, yet need outside source material to write the other three parts. Those outside sources provide information for which they're paid. In this example they are a clinic, a university and the mechanic down the street. I then deliver a speech to a selected audience. I am paid for the speech. The audience then relates this information to various segments of their organizations. This includes staff at the clinics, professors at universities and a particular automobile company.

Every company wants to believe they are progressive. More products, more sales, etc.. Likewise, you'll show your progression with added skills and how the better product(you) will add value to the company. Show that you are able to spread valuable information to the right markets(co-workers, clients, etc.) and you'll have a ready audience.

The 'So What' Test

For each part of your résumé— for the objective, summary of qualifications, experience, education and any other section you include, you must test the strength of your presentation. Read each sentence or statement, skill or ability and ask 'So what?'. If your answer provides more information than is in the statement, rewrite the statement. Add clarity to your vision. Analyze and refine your thoughts and written words over and over again.

Consider the following example:

Before: "Rewrote training manual for sales office."

So what?:   "Training used to go on for three weeks. Now it's two weeks, that's what!"

After: "Rewrote training manual, resulted in moving sales staff into field 35% faster."

Where possible, quantify your actions. Use dollar and percentage figures.

Never Never Land

Never include the following on your résumé:

1. Your current salary
2. What you expect for a salary
3. Full references, including names and addresses
4. Your photograph
5. Information about your spouse or children
6. Your marital status
7. Your health or weight
8. Any handicaps

And do not staple, glue or seal your résumé into a binder or folder.

For Recent College Graduates

If you have limited or no job experience, use the following as guidelines:

1. Addresses you use must list where contact can most easily be made. You may use two or sometimes three addresses for contact. Include any attention names, if other than your own. Match appropriate telephone numbers to addresses.
2. For your college, include the name, city, state and degree received. List only the year when the degree was awarded.
3. Highlight any honors awarded.
4. Include fluency in language(s).
5. Show specific skills you used in college, such as word processing, software applications, office machines, etc..
6. Do not disregard even a limited job experience. Include summer jobs, volunteer work, co–op work as an intern, assistance in research, etc..
7. Identify those valuable extracurricular activities. Perhaps you were in the debating club, a school newspaper or yearbook, an elected official, etc..
8. Show extensive travel if you can show benefit to the future employer.

When reviewing your résumé, remember these rules:

1. Does each part of the résumé pass the 'So what?' test?
2. Are numbers and percentages used wherever possible?
3. Have you used past tense throughout the details? Using action verbs to begin each power statement suggests an individual who'll contribute to the company and get the job done.
4. Have you used results–oriented language?
5. Have you stayed away from the jargon associated with a single profession?

Short, strong and powerful statements of skills, contributions and abilities should be incorporated throughout your résumé. For example, they might begin as follows:

Organized schedules to...
Identified 2 flaws in system by...
Tracked cleanup effort for...
Interviewed 4 possible candidates who...
Analyzed data so that...

Resolved conflict when...
Met auditing requirements which...
Excelled in interdepartmental competition and...
Rewarded for new product development with...
Contributed to special project that...
Mapped a plan so that...
Proofed department publication, finding...
Trained 3 supervisors who...
Assisted development of...
Travelled from...
Submitted proposal that was...
Represented division at...
Selected as project manager after...
Promoted within 6 months due to...
Explored new ways to...
Learned new software program in order to...
Discovered discrepancies which, when resolved,...
Studied new method of...
Received feedback, which, when analyzed,...
Travelled to leadership conference where...
Challenged support staff to exceed, resulting in...
Achieved dominant position as...
Surpassed departmental goals when...
Developed schedules which saved...
Systematized record system and cut down...
Sensed new market development, gaining...
Set strategy for selling new baked goods, resulting in...
Set monthly goals for trainees who...
Coordinated rotation of shelf stock, eliminating need for...
Organized travel tours for...
Compared software packages to decide on...
Evaluated new employee performance to determine...
Finished priority assignment before...
Advised pharmacy on distribution of...
Built new test model of...
Installed conveyor belt which reduced...
Made innovative wooden toys promoting...
Wrote brochure for medical supply firm which generated...
Spoke at manufacturing convention, addressing concerns of...
Prepared initial inventory for...
Tested prototype in 2 markets, gaining advantage of...

Identified best research method for...
Observed laboratory experiment critical to...
Assembled log home in partnership with...

When you express your strengths, do so in a language appropriate for your audience. If you abbreviate titles, functions or anything else, be sure those abbreviations are industry standards. The abbreviations should not be particular only to your past employer(s).

You'll only get hired if you can prove, in their language, that they need you and the valuable skills you'll bring with you.

Format

Each section of your résumé must be given a uniform style of language.

I suggest you use the present tense for the job objective and summary of qualifications. Use the past tense for everything else.

Do not use the word 'I' in your résumé. Do not use the phrase 'responsible for'. 'Responsible for' doesn't tell the reader anything. Do we assume you were 'responsible for' and failed? Did you succeed? Did you surpass goals by 20%? Similarly, please do not use the word 'interface'. When you 'interface', do you accomplish anything? Show the accomplishments.

Let's look at a before and after example:

Before

Abbott Co.   September, 1983 - Oct. 1989
Phoenix, Arizona

Assistant Researcher

- analyzed specimens to help project managers
-- I won an award for best research methods

- proposal for new research methods was accepted by the company

- was willing to work overtime when special jobs came in with priority status

After

Abbott Company, Phoenix, AZ   **1983–1989**
Research Assistant

- Analyzed specimens, enabling project managers to determine results.

- Proposed and implemented new research methods, shortening review process by 15%.

- Honored with award for outstanding contributions to division.

- Worked overtime to complete critical jobs with priority deadlines.

Bullets

You saw how bullets (•) were used in our 'After' example. Bullets allow the reader to identify separate strengths and skills. Compare the clean, bulleted examples with the dashed 'Before' examples. The bullets suggest strength and clarity. The dashes, as well as the varied spacing, suggest a section from a poorly crafted term paper.

Examples

You'll find some examples of bullets for twenty different professions or job titles. These bullets are not meant to be copied. Yours will be strengthened with numbers and percentages, highlighting specific savings and profits the company realized because of your efforts. Use the examples as a starting point to further refine your own contributions.

Auditor

- Uncovered lack of proper procedures costing company at least $90,000 per year. Wrote procedures and eliminated losses.

- Developed statistical analysis report, allowing managers to track variances of receivables by 1% increments.

- Honored with membership in The Henson Group, whose ranks are filled with peers who review and recommend only 25 new memberships per year.

- Monitored implementation of new audit standards.

Banker

- Trained 8 managers, focusing on client contact initiative.

- Submitted weekly appraisals of branches to home office.

- Initiated review process of high-risk mortgage applicants, reducing losses by 40%.

- Named liaison to auditors during review process of Operations. Explained and resolved discrepancies.

- Supervised 35 staff members in Operations group, in Corporate Reorganization and Income Collection.

Biologist

- Chosen over 12 other candidates to conduct graduate research with noted biologist.

- Coordinated activities of interns for 3 projects in process. Cut overtime requirements for 15 staff members by 25%.

- Participated in department analysis of $50,000 equipment purchase.

- Maintained confidential files, available to secured personnel only.

- Applied for and received funding for research experiment. Supervised 3 associates through project completion.

Computer Systems Analyst

- Collected data from all levels of management to create new program. Reduced work costs by 22%.

- Wrote working specifications for 5 junior programmers to follow. Cut overall programming time by 18%.

- Developed policy for affiliates to follow for submitting enhancement requests. Shortened response by 2 weeks.

- Devised new secured lock on access to critical data.

- Automated payroll department. Created direct deposit linkage. Defined new job descriptions for 12 positions.

Deli Worker

- Encouraged loyal customers to try new products, adding 6 permanent items to list within 4 months.

- Wrote product advertisements on company computer for in-house sales.

- Handled credit card orders for special corporate accounts. Increased usage of service, adding $1,200 per month in sales.

- Controlled inventory. Maintained best record in regional area for prevention of spoilage.

- Developed luncheon menu for call-in orders. Increased business on this high-profit market by 50%.

English Teacher

- Prepared database to store information on students. Analyzed strengths and weaknesses. Developed new methods which raised grades of 35% of students.

- Organized special events to local organizations. Emphasized local history on 5 outings.

- Published article, winning best investigative award.

- Set up itineraries for foreign exchange students. Participated in program, increasing students by 20% per year for 5 years, showing highest success rate in state.

Graphic Designer

- Supplied all graphics for company publication reaching work force of 2200 managers and technicians.

- Assisted in layout of major corporate publication. Helped distribute publication to 55 community groups and 7 government offices throughout area.

- Catalogued 300 in–house designs on computer, according to use by client base.

- Supported Vice President during presentations to 5 largest clients.

- Kept assignments current, assigning weekly schedules to all freelance support.

Health Services Professional

- Reviewed policies for hospital admittance. Made changes which reduced processing time by 20%.

- Devised new on–call procedures that benefited both patients and staff.

- Recruited nurse staff from other hospitals. Developed schedules that reduced turnover by 40%.

- Implemented controls over administrative stations, reducing paperwork obligations by 15%

Hotel Industry

- Updated and maintained customer files on computer system. Cut check–in time for previous clients by 50%.

- Authorized expenditures for refurbishment of 200 rooms. Lowered projected expenses by $125,000.

- Prepared monthly profit and loss statement for President.

- Revised and maintained cycling of carport. Returned cars to clients 40% faster.

- Identified safe and attractive sites in city and surrounding areas for tour groups. Surveyed tours and found 85% used service and would recommend hotel to future groups.

Insurance

- Developed procedures which uncovered fraudulent claims. Recovered $45,000 for division.

- Wrote manual for checking potential high–risk clients.

- Promoted to contracts coordinator after one year. Hired for new position 30% faster than department standard.

- Interviewed high–risk applicants, screening according to company policies. Reduced high–risk cases by 45%.

- Reviewed statements and invoices of field agents. Authorized payments of miscellaneous expenses. Tracked and reduced expenses by $60,000.

Machinist

- Arranged new working specifications for safer environment. Reduced first year injuries by 75%.

- Taught new employees how to use equipment. Wrote 3 operating manuals for each work process.

- Serviced 15 machines from other divisions. Maintained highest quality of equipment throughout region.

- Attended technical seminars to review equipment specs.Wrote 10–step simplified guideline for each machine introduced.

- Conducted 35 tours per year for visiting clients.

Medical Assistant

- Observed and recorded suggestions of visiting foreign staff. Incorporated improvements into daily work plans.

- Prepared slides for testing. Reduced turnaround by 2 days.

- Filed appropriate forms for compliance with government regulations.

- Wrote pamphlet on nutritional habits for inner–city youth. Distributed 30,000 copies to community centers.

- Wrote office procedures for part–time staff. Increased work assignments and reduced part–time staff count from 12 to 7.

Office Worker

- Added delinquent accounts to software program. Shortened collection period by 15 days.

- Sorted and filed customer orders according to priorities developed by owner. Bettered order fulfillment by 4 days.

- Organized computer back–up methods for 12 office employees. Tracked adherence to schedule weekly.

- Achieved highest output processing orders. Moved order requests to shipping 2 days ahead of defined standards.

- Developed a weekly status report on office supplies for 3 regions. Reduced task from 12 to 5 hours per week.

Public Relations

- Acted as liaison between company and community development program. Raised company profile in area, increasing corporate name recognition by 30%.

- Co–authored company literature sent to all high–level prospects. Increased mailings from 260 per quarter to 300 per month, a 200%+ increase.

- Booked national speakers for corporate–wide seminars. Added 45 new clients in 4 new regional markets.

- Hosted benefit for visiting European corporate staff. Entertained 22 colleagues. Attended functions at cultural centers and special events planned in their honor.

Photographer

- Won lead assignment on photographing a company exclusive. Photographs appeared in company annual report and 3 regional publications.

- Published in over 20 regional magazines and newspapers, as well as 3 national weeklies.

- Received award for best landscape photograph. Honored with plaque and reception by community organization.

- Assumed position of chief photographer after one year. Achieved position as newspaper increased readership from 325,000 to 460,000 per day.

- Produced 14 story ideas selected for lead photo essays.

Receptionist

- Developed system of prioritizing schedules for staff.

- Arranged travel of 5 marketing managers. Reduced scheduling discrepancies by 75%.

- Handled all queries of public regarding department. Responded to 50 varied requests per month.

- Worked with computer consulting group to set up networking environment for all Marketing Managers to access records. Cut requests for paper records by 80%.

- Assisted architect in redesign of 25 support staff offices.

Secretary

- Prepared conference rooms to meet high–level standards of visiting foreign dignitaries.

- Bought software and created master file of client names, addresses, etc. to be used by 12 salespeople.

- Controlled supplies inventory. Reduced expenses from $18,000 to $11,000 per year.

- Promoted to Personal Assistant to Vice President after 6 months.

- Recommended copier, fax and personal computer purchases. Received approval on expenditures for $35,000 of equipment.

Sales

- Created new market for XYZ product, increasing sales by 30%. Added 8% to net revenues of the department.

- Coordinated promotional campaign, gaining $44,000 in first year profits.

- Managed sales penetration of new territories. Identified and sold in 5 new markets.

- Achieved highest yearly sales among 18 sales managers. Surpassed required quota by 35% each year for 3 years.

Telephone Company

- Serviced new clients, reducing sign–on processing time by 50%.

- Supervised 12 work–study students for two semesters. Signed 3 students on for permanent assignments.

- Contributed leadership position to company–sponsored outreach program. Conducted tours for 900 citizens.

- Set up and maintained records of 1000 customer complaints. Reviewed response procedures. Introduced action plan which lowered complaints by 60%.

Travel Agent

- Used computer software, fax and copiers to speed bookings and mailing confirmations. Processed 1500 reservations up to 20% faster.

- Created monthly flyers sent to previous clients, highlighting special weekend packages. Increased weekend bookings by 40%.

- Booked daily schedules for politician and staff. Added other government leads and increased yearly gross earnings by $20,000.

- Promoted new and profitable tour packages. Brought in $5,000 in higher monthly net revenue.

Your Name, Address and Telephone Number

You really only have two choices for placing your name, address and telephone number on your résumé. You may place it at the top center or at the top right portion of the page.

Placing the résumé heading at the top left portion is not advisable. Consider the résumé reader. Your résumé may be in a folder with 50 others. Or worse, a binder. A three–hole punch may put a hole through the header information if you've placed it at the top left portion of the page. Don't tuck your identify away where it won't be noticed.

Dates on Your Résumé

Use years only on your résumé. There are two reasons you should use years only. First, the reader can immediately see that all years are covered. The interview will proceed uninterrupted. Second, if using months, you've distracted the readers attention to superfluous information. Does a month define an accomplishment? What if a month from 1981 is unaccounted for? You'll be asked about 'missing work history' that may not be easy to explain.

The distraction of including months on your résumé does not help you in any way and should be eliminated.

Excessive Language and Style of Content

Beware of excessive language. Do not reinforce a phrase needlessly. Do present each job block to your best advantage.

If the reader comes upon a paragraph–laden résumé in her stack, chances are you'll be passed over. Follow the examples from the power statements you created in the chapter 'Focusing on Strengths'. Use your short, powerful statements. With the résumé, less is more. If you've crammed every detail into the résumé, what are you going to say during the interview?

Repetition of Words and Facts

Each of your short, powerful statements should begin with a different action verb. Use them to sell your story but don't use them more than once. Buy a thesaurus. For a quick reference, refer to the sample list of action verbs in the chapter entitled 'Worksheets'.

You'll be able to find similar action verbs to use. If you used 'devised' to begin one statement, use 'planned' in another. Using the same words throughout your document does not show progression.

Similarly, let the facts speak for themselves but speak only once. If you have had three jobs where you've used a skill, show that skill only once. For instance, if you can type 70 words per minute, list that skill once. Still, similar skills may often be used to show progression.

Consider this example.

Review the skills Sheila has gained in the last ten years. She can type 70 words per minute(wpm). She can use a personal computer. She can fax documents. Since she'll be starting with her most recent job and moving backwards, here's how the bullets might look on her résumé:

Most Recent Job

• Bought fax computer software, enabling staff to send faxes directly from computers. Scheduled non–critical material for evening transmission, reducing monthly telephone charges by 12%.

Next Most Recent Job

• Volunteered to research and determine best computer hardware and software for department. Moved recommendations to actual purchases, resulting in transferral of 80% of files to an automated environment.

Next Most Recent Job

- Outperformed typing requirements of 50 wpm, consistently realizing 70 wpm.

In almost all cases, she did not learn every skill at one time only. Sheila progressed. Show the progression.

Reinforcing Phrases Needlessly

Make your statements short and sweet. Clarity sells.

Write 'difficult' instead of 'really difficult'. Write 'set by management priorities' instead of 'priorities set according to the decisions of management'. Write '$5 million' instead of 'five million dollars'. Review every part of your résumé. Ask yourself two questions:

1. Can I shorten what I've written?
2. Can I say it better?

Presenting "Job Blocks" to Best Advantage

Think of your résumé as a benefits statement. When you're buying a new car, does the salesperson proudly highlight the floor mats first? No, of course not. And neither should you.

When you write your short, powerful statements under each job heading, prioritize. Prioritize statements according to the most important benefits you can sell to the employer.

Sell the platinum. Sell the gold. Sell the silver. In that order.

Also, give more emphasis to the bulleted statements which are impressive. Give three or four lines to a great accomplishment. Summarize what benefits you the least. The number of bullets for each job may follow the same rules. Perhaps you'll give four bullets to your most recent, most important job. The last position you list may only have one bullet of information.

The "I hate to do it" Factor

An important part of composing your résumé is knowing what to leave out. As you reassess skills and gain new ones, you have to highlight those qualities that will get you the job that is most satisfying. Omitting some skills may give you certain advantages.

As you move up in your career, new skills will be used as old ones are retired. Just as the corporate executive will not maintain her speed on the manual typewriter from 20 years ago, you too will retire some of your skills. And as you move up, the things you dislike doing should be the primary things you retire.

The periods in your life that call for new résumés are the perfect times to redefine your career identify. First, we suggest that if you hate to do something you should leave it off your résumé. Second, the skills and details of your work and life history that you do not want to take to your next job should be omitted.

The more specific you are in addressing exactly what you want, the more likely it is you'll get it.

Chronological, Functional or Targeted Résumés?

As the years pass, new styles and formats are introduced as the 'best' methods for presenting your résumé. We find the three listed above as the most frequently used examples. This book recommends only the chronological format and we'll explain why.

Just as the most highly qualified individual may not get the job, the résumé with the most skills listed may not win either. Why does this happen? Confusion.

When did you do what in your career? This skill has the most benefits for us. Were you doing it on the last job or the one before that? Were you doing it 15 years ago? The functional and targeted résumés may not readily answer those questions. The chronological résumé will.

The chronological résumé relates skills and qualifications to work history. Using this format you will show progression in your career. You'll show that you were rewarded with promotions and increasing responsibilities. You'll show what is potentially relevant to the employer while still presenting a full case for all your talents.

The functional résumé provides skills and qualifications but makes the association to specific work history difficult to decipher. However talented you are, have you learned new skills over the last few years? The functional résumé keeps the reader guessing. Are you hiding certain facts? Is there any gap in your history that I should try to figure out? Have you buried a detail or relationship that I should try to discover? The reader may pass over your résumé instead of guessing at the answers.

The targeted résumé provides those exact skills and specifications for a certain job or company. What if the job or company changes the requirements of the position a week after receiving your résumé? Even though you may have the skills newly required, don't expect the company to come after you for additional information. What if they had a higher paying job to offer but you didn't qualify because you left off one of your skills? In every case, all aspects of the job search are your responsibility. A well-rounded presentation is better than one which includes certain details and excludes others. Remember, a multi-talented individual is better off than a specialist who excels in one area and is dysfunctional in all the others.

Sadly, you won't know the full reason for losing out on a job opportunity. Why lose because you didn't list skills, history and contributions you have an abundance of?

Now, turn to the next chapter. You'll be able to review 25 examples of résumés, covering many different occupations. Some of the bullets given are from actual résumés people have used, some are composites and others are meant to stimulate your own ideas. Whether or not you'd want to put a similar statement on your résumé, use the formats and the bullets shown to help you identify all the great things you've done in your life.

Résumé Examples

A Special Note:

You'll find that each of the following résumés is surrounded by a black line border. This border is not meant to suggest the actual sheet of paper, for in that case the content of the résumé would be too close to the papers' edge. The actual size of this book, 8 1/2 x 11, represents the actual size of a résumé.

Rather, the black line border is included to show you how white space is used and how various parts of similar material is balanced. For example, notice how dates are shown in the same position throughout each document. Also, use the black border line to see how bold and italicized typefaces are interspersed throughout each document in a balanced fashion.

Remember to use a similar, pleasing design with your own résumé. By now you know how critically important the "look" is to your success.

Another Special Note:

Each of the following 25 résumés is a 1–page document. There has been no mention of the preferred number of pages to a résumé until now. This is because we feel you'll use as many pages as you feel appropriate until you come to understand a very important rule. Here it is:

- Unless it is not important to you to get a job, a 1–page résumé is your only choice.

This is an awfully simple rule, but one that is very difficult to follow. Start with however many pages you feel necessary, then simplify, simplify and simplify some more.

Remember, you've got about 30 seconds to sell your qualifications initially. With a 2–page résumé the interviewer will give 14 seconds to each page(after all, 2 seconds are lost to turning the page).

Résumé Paper

This book shows résumés on white paper. The paper stock you use will be very important to your success. Whether you do your own résumé or use a résumé preparation service, be sure to insist on high quality, heavyweight paper with a good percentage of cotton fibre(25% or higher).

For most jobs, paper may be off–white, white, ivory, natural or gray in color. We prefer ivory or natural as it sets the document off from most other office correspondence. We use gray more for scientists and engineers than for other professions. Designers, promotional advertisers, etc., may decide to use a more esoteric method of presentation. Analyze your market and respond to it accordingly.

Now, move on to the résumé examples and get ideas for your own résumé presentation.

Good luck!

	Your Name	Your Name
	Street Address	Street Address
	City, State, Zip Code	City, State, Zip Code
	Telephone Number (or)	Telephone Number

Job Objective:

Summary of Qualifications:

Experience: Company Name, City, State   Year(s)
Title, Department   *Year(s)(if holding multiple job titles with 1 organization)*

•

•

•

Title, Department   *Year(s)*

•

•

Company Name, City, State   *Year(s)*
Title, Department   *Year(s)(if holding multiple job titles with 1 organization)*

•

•

Education: School Name, City, State   Year(s) Attended
Degree: Major, Minor(use GPA if high and recently graduated)
Or: Course of Study or Certificates Awarded
And: Honors and Awards

Professional Affiliations: Name of Organization, City, State   *Year(s)*
(only if appropriate to your job search)
Your Status

• *Highlight of responsibilities, if appropriate*

(Of course you'll supply references, so don't bother with a section entitled 'References'.

Your Name
Street Address
City, State, Zip Code
Telephone Number

Job Objective:

Qualified By:

Experience: Company Name, City, State   Year(s)
Title, Department   Year(s)(if holding multiple
job titles with 1 organization)

-

-

-

Title, Department   Year(s)

-

-

Company Name, City, State   Year(s)
Title, Department   Year(s)(if holding multiple
job titles with 1 organization)

-

Title, Department   Year(s)

Education: School Name, City, State   Year(s) Attended
Degree: Major, Minor(use GPA if high and recently graduated)
Or: Course of Study or Certificates Awarded
And: Honors and Awards

Systems Applications:
- Programming Languages(specify)
- Hardware used(specify)
- Software(specify)

Languages:
- Fluency in...

Professional Affiliations: (only if appropriate to your job search)   Year(s)
Name of Organization, City, State
Your Status

- Highlight of responsibilities, if appropriate

(Of course you'll supply references, so don't bother with a section entitled 'References'.

Peter Stockwell
22 East 57th Street
New York, NY 10022
Tel: (212) 753–4629

Job Objective: Supporting senior management by handling schedules and using all office technologies.

Summary of Qualifications: Using computer software applications and other technologies to handle record maintenance, business trip scheduling and all word processing for management team.

Experience: **James Publishing, New York, NY**   1990–1991
Senior Administrative Assistant

- Handled record maintenance on Macintosh computer, maintaining name and address files, business scheduling and other important tasks with various software.

- Resolved conflicting schedules of 4 managers, ensuring proper coverage at home office for walk–in clients.

- Designed new forms for weekly project reports, cutting 2 hours of paperwork per week for 4 managers. Received award recognition for adding 8 hours to client sales time.

- Identified inadequacies in ordering office supplies. Centralized ordering, using alternative vendors and reducing monthly costs by $1,400.

Danta Resources, Boston, MA   1987–1989
Administrative Assistant

- Conducted all office tasks for a research and consulting firm. Used in–house accounting system, fax machine, copying equipment and personal computer to expedite all assignments.

- Updated monthly budget report for senior management. Created new back–up system for reports, enabling authorized parties to conduct comparison reviews of sales for a 2–year period.

Systems Skills: IBM, using Lotus 1–2–3
Macintosh, using Microsoft Word and Microsoft Excel

Angela Walton
2812 Pennsylvania Avenue, NW
Washington, DC 20007
Tel: (202) 965–0037

Objective: Leading project teams in defining the markets for large corporate accounts.

**Summary of
Qualifications:** Expertise in developing regional markets for high–priority accounts. Success at setting up desktop publishing units to create profitable client presentations.

**Professional
Background:**

DeWitt Group, **Washington, DC**   **1987–1991**
Marketing Director

- Analyzed and recommended strategies for $500,000+ regional campaigns. Created project teams to tailor individual client presentations. Used kits and desktop publishing slide shows as part of sales program. Added 15 new accounts in first year.

- Oversaw development of new training department. Determined systems software needs of 40 staff members. Tailored training schedules according senior management directives. Spent $150,000 in first year costs and realized $400,000 in proven additional earnings.

- Worked with consulting group to develop interactive account information. Planned, with security pass codes, access to selected materials for 3 field offices.

- Received senior management approval to hire 2 systems professionals and act as their manager. Met with clients to refine and develop programs for further specialization. Added $600,000+ to gross earnings through team effort.

Wallace Howard, Inc., **New York, NY**   **1980–1986**
Marketing Manager

- Supervised 2 assistant planners. Prepared monthly reports for executive office. Wrote comparison reports on effective advertising campaigns.

- Created marketing brochures for 8 different business groups. Used desktop publishing software to create individualized written reports for high–profile accounts.

Education: Trinity College, Washington, DC   **1979**
B.F.A., Visual Communications

Dean Volpe
493 Sutter Street
San Francisco, CA 94102
Tel: (415) 421–5628

Objective: To succeed as an Operations Manager in a banking environment.

**Qualifications
Summary:** Management of Income Collection, Corporate Reorganization,
and DTC settlement. Consistent support to Fed Reserve settlement.

**Professional
Background:** **American Bank, San Francisco, CA** 1985–1991
Operations Manager

- Managed 2 Operations officers, 4 Supervisors and 40 staff in
  Income Collection, Corporate Reorganization and DTC.

- Designed better methods for daily Income Collection settlements.
  Posted income to accounts without discrepancies by comparing
  account totals with net received before night settlement.

- Oversaw reduction of failed trades in DTC by 80%, reducing
  broker claims significantly.

- Assisted in debugging systems software for in–house trust system.
  Remedied 6 bugs, allowing for new automation of 2 functions.
  Reduced manual processing for operations group, saving 60 staff
  hours per week.

- Selected as Operations liaison for Personal Trust division as
  officers were trained on new accounting system.

Canton Facility Bank, Canton, MA 1981–1984
Assistant Manager, Corporate Reorganization and Income Collection

- Read specifications of 3 trust accounting service bureau systems.
  Recommended 1 system, saving $380,000 in project costs while
  maintaining objective for highest overall quality for product.

- Oversaw salary review process. Determined raise allocations
  to be used by 2 Operations officers for staff. Wrote 7 reviews and
  approved 30 others.

- Introduced part–time and flexible work hours. Reduced total man
  hours in division by 12% without layoffs.

Education: University of Massachusetts, Boston, MA 1981
B.S., Operations Management

Georgia Bush
500 Canyon Road
Santa Fe, NM 87501
Tel: (505) 982–8814

Job Objective: *Specializing in managing high net–worth trust accounts.*

Summary of
Qualifications: *Creating management teams to provide all services to Estates.*
Proven support to revocable and non–revocable trust officers.

Experience: **Diablo Trust, Santa Fe, NM**   **1980–1991**
Senior Trust Officer

- Managed 362 accounts. Handled all matters related to the
  accounts and directed work assignments of 2 administrative
  assistants.

- Organized monthly reports for senior management, showing
  and explaining expense fluctuations in division. Submitted and
  received approval for setting up computerized reporting,
  reducing preparation time by 50%.

- Assisted in direction of marketing campaign to add $50 million
  in new trust accounts over a 1–year period. Surpassed goal and
  reached $85 million in allocated time period.

- Participated in conversion of trusts from in–house to service–
  bureau accounting system. Formed 1 of 2 core teams for conversion,
  handling all administrative issues. Converted 8,200 accounts.

Santa Fe Bank, Santa Fe, NM   **1973–1979**
Trust Officer

- Settled disagreements on operating procedures between 2
  departments. Defined working roles for each; wrote new job
  descriptions for 28 employees. Submitted data to personnel for
  salary structure rewrites.

- Represented 6% of staff and administered 12% of accounts,
  in both number and value.

- Volunteered to act as liaison to development area while
  programming changes were made to trust accounting system.

Education: **University of New Mexico**   **1973**
B.S., Economics

Achievements: **Who's Who of American Women**   **1977–1991**

Marilyn Kennedy
144 South Commerce Street
Centreveille, MD 21617
Tel: (301) 758–9538

Job Objective: *Supporting senior management in all high–pressure situations.*

Overview of Qualifications: *Preparing reports and schedules to streamline travel for senior managers. Handling critical correspondence and managing recordkeeping for executive and legal review.*

Work Experience:

Wiggins Consulting Group, Centreville, MD — 1986–1991
Executive Secretary

- Produced monthly client mailings, increasing prospect calls for manager by 15% in first quarter.

- Assisted district attorney in preparation of case work. Expedited 35 cases per month, creating new record maintenance files which reduced manual processing an average of 12 days.

- Composed daily transcripts of meetings between clients and President. Maintained computerized file of 800 transcripts, submitting duplicated disk files to legal department each month.

- Spent 5–year period handling 8 work assignments for 2 company Presidents, 3 Vice Presidents and various members of other executive offices.

Delphi Regional Resources, Washington, DC — 1979–1985
Executive Secretary

- Joined President and executive group on 2–month overseas trip to record all formal and informal conversations with various staff of company in process of being merged. Transcribed all notes into one journal for executive and legal review.

- Handled all correspondence for Executive Office. Answered material as appropriate and forwarded the rest. Cut mail review by executive staff by a total of 4 hours per week.

- Reorganized executive support staff so that senior officers would draw on multiple individuals versus having one dedicated support person. Resulted in returning assignments to group as much as 15% faster.

Education:

Bowie State College, Bowie, MD — 1988–1991
Courses in Communications Media

Systems Skills: **Various desktop publishing programs on both IBM and Macintosh systems.**

129

John Prickett
68 East Walton Street
Chicago, IL 60611
Tel: (312) 337–4462

Job Objective: Developing individualized programs for human resources training and development.

Highlighted
Qualifications: Training middle and senior level managers on developing corporate policies. Presenting seminars and lectures to participants throughout the manufacturing industry.

Professional
Background:

Hoskins Manufacturing, Chicago, IL *1983–1991*
Regional Training Director, Corporate Human Resources

- Presented seminar entitled 'Manufacturing and the Workforce: Into the 90's'. Edited material for corporate publication, distributing 35,000 copies to clients and other prospective users.

- Recruited speakers with highest name recognition value for corporate events. Allocated $200,000 per year for up to 30 speeches, with corporate–set limits of $10,000 per speech.

- Travelled throughout Midwest region, meeting with affiliates and high–priority clients. Ensured compliance to home office regulations. Spent 2 days per week reviewing affiliate practices, visiting sites and verifying adherence to policies.

- Wrote source material and taught senior–level trainers how to present a proper corporate image to all new recruits. Updated material twice yearly, ensuring validity for 550 new hires per year.

- Assisted in corporate relocation of 50 staff members. Interviewed each to address individual and company concerns. Realized an 85% success rate for regional plan for relocation.

Bon–Tel Systems, Chicago, IL *1975–1982*
Development Officer

- Directed 2 assistants and secretary in coordinating program attendance at 8 regional sites per year. Created agendas for 3–day programs. Opened each program with introduction and first 2–hour speech on various topics.

- Devised backup plans and schedules to handle any cancellations, from speaking arrangements to course materials presented to participants. Used backup material on 3 occasions with no delays or problems.

Education: **Northwestern University** *1975*
B.S., Political Science

Jonathan Adler
1845 Chestnut Street
Philadelphia, PA 19103
Tel: (215) 563–8519

Objective: To pursue research and development as an electrical engineer.

Background Summary: Proven ability to direct test programs, ensuring conformity to industry standards and client requirements. Analyzing and verifying contractual obligations with outside contractors.

Experience: *Chandler Engineering, Inc., Philadelphia, PA*   1987–1991
Engineer

- Negotiated contracts with independent contractors. Agreed to two–tier method of payment based on speed and validation of quality results. Resulted in maintaining costs while completing assignments 10% ahead of schedules.

- Participated in joint venture between 3 firms and government agency for engineering contracts. Adjusted estimates through research efforts of 6–person team. Realized additional revenue of $300,000.

- Implemented projects to develop advanced security systems circuitry. Introduced 3 modifications that cut unit costs by 20%.

- Developed 4 modifications to wiring system for prototype aircraft. Received approval to test each, separately and together. Resulted in proposed changes to certain aircraft, pending further approval.

- Organized company source materials and client contracts and bought systems software to store information. Set up desktop stations for personnel and worked with trainers to teach personnel how to access material and share time on common network.

- Supervised staff of 12 engineers of various levels.

Advanced Engineering Systems, Philadelphia, PA   1984–1986
Engineer

- Coordinated installations at 6 client sites. Ensured that all aspects of contracts were completed. Installed 2 clients on schedule and 4 clients ahead of schedule.

- Directed staff in the production of control equipment.

Education: *University of Lowell, Lowell, MA*   1984
B.S., Electrical Engineering

Marguerite Brown
197 Bellevue Avenue
Newport, RI 02840
Tel: (401) 849–6255

Job Objective: **Specializing in marketing analysis for new mass–market products.**

Qualified By: In–depth knowledge of regional distribution networks.
Proven ability to analyze short–term results to determine
long–term profitable strategies.

**Professional
Experience:**

Newport Development Corporation, Newport, RI   1986–1991
Senior Marketing Director

- Organized senior management teams to streamline distribution
  channels for 18 affiliates. Reduced processing functions, cut number
  of staff in production lines and delivered product to shipping
  3 days faster. Netted over $1,000,000 in annual savings.

- Supervised program which placed new employees into production
  lines. Produced results which maintained speed of facility, added
  4 hours to production cycles at no extra employee costs and reduced
  rebates to customers by $40,000.

- Set up administrative offices for newly formed subsidiary.
  Planned work areas for President, 3 managers and 55 support staff.

- Researched and bought 10 p.c.'s that were put on same network.
  Added fax modems and all supporting office equipment. Worked out
  corporate discount plan, reducing purchase costs by $9,000.

Boston Bottling Company, Inc., Somerville, MA   1983–1985
Regional Manager

- Initiated audit of monthly sales reports. Found discrepancies
  amongst 5 dealers. Recovered $55,000 in underreported income and
  put in place monthly audit procedures to prevent any recurring losses.

- Modified production facility at 2 bottling plants. Added 6 hours to
  production cycles to allow for 24–hour schedules. Adjusted work hours
  and introduced flex–time, resulting in no additions to staff.

- Moved sales staff to new offices 40 days ahead of schedule.
  Kept viable working conditions at old and new locations so
  no disruption in client sales would take place.

Education: **Green Mountain College**, Poultney, VT   1983
B.S., Retail Management

Deborah York
55 South Main Street
Essex, CT 06426
Tel: (203) 767–0499

Objective: Using systems skills to gain high–volume sales from large corporate accounts.

Summarized Qualifications: Working knowledge of system hardware and software as benefits Fortune 500–type accounts. Ability to demonstrate dozens of programs which streamline numerous office functions.

Work Experience: *Best Computer Sales, Stonington, CT* **1988–1991**
Sales Manager

- Created 2 displays for corporate sales presentation at industry convention. Realized 300% increase over previous year sales. Won convention award for best and most ingenious display.

- Developed special program for clients making over $10,000 in yearly purchases, providing cursory 1–day training seminars on certain applications for up to 12 members of their staff. Won over $350,000 in contracts as a result of special program.

- Participated as committee member, selecting new software to add to sales packages. Met once each month to analyze and select up to 5 new products.

O'Neill and Briggs, Inc., Hartford, CT **1983–1987**
Systems Analyst

- Maintained name and address files for 3400 clients. Directed project to identify regional markets and create segmented mailing lists for quarterly direct mail campaigns.

- Converted 22–person office from manual to computerized environment. Set up network, common printing areas and direct fax capabilities.

- Purchased 7 software programs to streamline various office functions. Conducted training classes for all users

Additional Experience: Spent 1 year travelling throughout Europe and Japan to determine **1982**
how business systems software was used to streamline office functions.

Education: *Sacred Heart University, Bridgeport, CT* **1981**
Courses in Computer Science

Software Applications: Working knowledge of dozens of IBM and Macintosh–compatible software programs, with expertise in numerous business management applications.

Philip Graham
11 Main Street
Limington, ME 04049
Tel: (207) 793–3852

Job Objective:	Streamlining processing in contract change, adding to customer satisfaction and increasing profits.

Summary of Qualifications:

Joining quality assurance initiatives to introduce the best methods of processing documents through contract change division. Using expertise in insurance regulations to lead staff, submit plans for improved products and gain approval from senior management to maximize profits.

Professional Background:

Gannett Insurance Company, Portland, ME　　　　　　　1987–1991
Specialist

- Headed focus group for quality control project initiated by Division Executive. Submitted weekly status reports on successes of 8–member group.

- Enacted 15 changes to flow of contract documents, from receipt to stamping, prioritizing material, field calls, research and contract change. Cut processing schedule from 7 to 4 business days.

- Served as contact between home office and 12 field offices in contract change division. Wrote amendments to policies and ensured turnaround in 4 business days.

- Supervised 7 administrators. Attained 24–hour turnaround for all high–priority documents, as determined by senior management.

- Maintained direct contact with 30 agents.

Ryan Insurance, San Francisco, CA　　　　　　　　　　1985–1986
Analyst

- Introduced findings from 2–week program(held in Phoenix, AZ) to senior management via written reports and technical spreadsheets. Streamlined 6 processing functions and saved 15 man hours per week throughout department.

- Trained new staff on appropriate working methods of office. Devised 3–part training method for new employees to validate and measure competency over initial 4–week period.

- Performed all job functions above departmental standards, earning 3 Achievement Awards over 4 years.

Education:	**San Francisco State University**　　　1985 *B.S., Accounting*

Elizabeth Pratt
14 Roxbury Street
Keene, NH 03431
Tel: (603) 357–9617

Job Objective: *Providing technical expertise to small companies intent on instituting systems programming to maximize efficiencies.*

Qualifications Summary: *Investigating technical developments in the computer industry, showing small and start–up firms how to benefit by converting manual processes to a computerized environment.*

Professional Experience:

Keene Programming Resources, Keene, NH   1988–1991
Technical Consultant

- Designed and subsequently implemented auxiliary plans for operating system during major power outages. Maintained services during 3 day outage, averting potential losses of $450,000.

- Calculated benefits of planned purchase of new system software for senior management at a start–up firm. Cancelled plans of purchase; $200,000 expenditure would have made for one–time $80,000 savings.

- Acted as primary support person in client support area for 6 months. Used knowledge of 5 programming languages to handle all immediate client concerns.

- Visited various client sites, averaging 6 per week, to ensure various applications were utilized properly. Met with senior management teams to correct inefficiencies and plan for new advancements.

Executive Placement, Inc., Peterborough, NH   1985–1987
Systems Programming Consultant

- Coordinated efforts of 4 affiliate banks to convert to 1 system for processing fees to the general ledger. Instituted controls for balancing funds and safeguarding against any improprieties.

- Assigned to 6–month project to review operating procedures at publishing firm. Rewrote guidelines for reconciling inventory, coding inventory to track cyclical sales and creating reports based on needs of senior managers. Saved company $360,000.

- Assisted investment firm in conversion of in–house system to a service bureau. Moved $8 billion in assets.

Education: **Dartmouth College, Hanover, NH**   1985
B.S., Computer Science

Alexander Tyson
80 Walton Avenue
Lexington, KY 40508
Tel: (606) 252–7463

Objective: Representing a corporation at client and community functions, achieving a positive corporate identity while promoting company goals.

Qualified By: Ability to give medium–sized companies a unique identity, using speaking engagements, company publications and client meetings to create specialized niches which lead to high profits.

Professional Background:

Manning Associates   *1990–1991*
Public Relations Officer

- Used corporate resources to join 5 community organizations together to create neighborhood development programs. Gained exposure in regional media(television, radio and newspaper). Surveyed for corporate name recognition after 6 months of program, showing increase from 31% to 65% in poll area(3 states).

- Spoke at community events, acting as corporate spokesperson. Delivered 25 speeches over 2–year period to 12 organizations.

- Escorted over 30 visitors through manufacturing plant each year. Explained equipment functionality and arranged demonstrations.

- Oversaw production of in–house journal. Arranged for cover art, line illustrations, charts and stories on a monthly basis. Produced 12 monthly issues as well as 2 special issues each year.

- Created quarterly newsletter directed at clients. Distributed 600 per month through sales force.

Transylvania University, Lexington, KY   *1987–1990*
Work Assignments

- Worked at 3 various assignments during school semesters. Used proficiencies on Macintosh computer to contribute at desktop publishing, word processing and spreadsheet analysis.

Education: **Transylvania University, Lexington, KY**   *1986–1990*
84 credits towards B.A. in History

Additional Accomplishments:

- Changed student newspaper from monthly to weekly as Editor. Gained enough area advertising to afford 3 new p.c.'s and 1 printer.

- Freelanced photo–essay assignment. Sold rights to publishing group for national distribution.

Matthew Young
386 Broadway
Cambridge, MA 02139
Tel: (617) 864–2281

Career Goals: Adding new skills in retail management, enhancing on proven ability to provide better client service while adding to company profits.

Summary of Qualifications: Creating better control procedures for inventory, identifying new methods of doing business that increase customer satisfaction. Making proven contributions that add to bottom–line profits.

Experience: **Peterson Hardware, Somerville, Ma** 1988–1991
Floor Manager

- Obtained and analyzed 5 quotes from shipping companies for local deliveries. Chose 2 new carriers, saving $350 per month in charges.

- Shipped packages within 1 business day of order receipt. Introduced new system which reduced backlogs completely.

- Added 40 new name and address files to computer database daily. Cross–referenced all files to find and eliminate duplicate records.

- Set up new packaging requirements for mail–order deliveries. Converted to all environmentally safe packing materials while reducing annual costs by $20,000.

- Prepared and stamped all incoming orders.

Temple Garden Supply, Worcester, MA 1986–1987
Cashier/Assistant

- Learned about all plants in stock, over 100 different items. Assisted as many as 200 customers per week, explaining proper garden care and suggesting various purchases. Maintained best sales record out of 5 assistants.

- Helped customers fill all gardening needs, from clothing to outdoor and indoor equipment purchases.

Education: **Worcester State College, Worcester, MA** 1987
Courses in Business Administration

Office Skills: In-house inventory processing system, copier equipment, fax machines, p.c.'s and various recordkeeping controls.

Doris Robinson
126 King Street
Charleston, SC 29401
Tel: (803) 723–2995

Objective: *Providing the best in management experience to a retail sales environment.*

Qualified By: *Achieving goals set by senior management teams to provide staff incentives for increasing market share. Consolidating operations, eliminating redundancies and setting long-term goals to produce exceptional profits.*

Professional Background:

Simpson Clothing Importers, Charleston, SC   1986–1991
Senior Sales Director

- Developed long–range goals for office support team. Created 5–step method for earning bonuses. Added $11,000 in earnings and distributed $2,200 in bonuses with experimental plan.

- Introduced experimental plan throughout organization. Added, over a 3–year time frame, over $500,000 in net profit while giving out $100,000 in bonuses. Reduced staff turnover, cut sick leave by 35% and placed company in 1st rank for profit per employee.

- Brought selected clients together with buyers to conduct quarterly information sessions. Realized introduction of 10 new product lines and increased net earnings 4%.

- Revamped office layout. Added 2 workers to each of 8 offices, reducing square footage costs by $29,000 per year

- Drew up plans to forecast cyclical earnings for 3 non–seasonal product lines. Directed production cycle to match earnings cycle. Saved $40,000 in inventorying costs.

The Tampa Group, Tampa, FL   1981–1985
Assistant Manager, Women's Apparel

- Undertook survey of all charge account clients, focusing on all lines of women's clothing. Worked with data entry group to tabulate results. Eliminated 4 lines of dresses, 2 lines of undergarments, and 3 lines of outerwear. Substituted other preferred lines which outsold former group by 75%.

- Won Achievement Award for revamping 3 departments in division. Received 10% bonus for adding significant profits.

Education: **University of South Carolina**   1981
B.S., Finance and Marketing

David Allison
5755 Kennett Pike
Wilmington, DE 19807
Tel: (302) 656–0110

Job Objective: Providing excellent computer–support skills to managers in a business environment.

Qualifications Summary: Excelling at data processing and desktop publishing for management staff. Using software applications to make for more efficient handling of management assignments.

Work Experience:

Wilmington Consulting, Inc., Wilmington, DE   **1989–1991**
Secretary

- Produced sales lead documents for staff, faxing up to 25 per day to various regional locations. Provided initial data concerning client names, addresses, contact methods and potential purchases.

- Transcribed all meeting notes for 3 research projects going on concurrently. Formatted material in 2 ways, 1st as original transcription for legal department and 2nd as spreadsheet documents for tracking by Executive Committee.

- Used Microsoft Word and Microsoft Excel to produce all documents for 1 research project, Lotus 1–2–3 for other 2 projects.

- Acted as secretary to 4 Regional Managers.

Wilson Accountants, Wilmington, DE   **1985–1988**
Secretary

- Received material from 2 divisions, comprising 9 departments, for inclusion in monthly staff journal. Used Aldus PageMaker to format material into 4 pages. Included text, line art and scanned images as determined by 2 Vice Presidents.

- Asked to assist in creation of new unit to handle all printed material published by corporation. Worked with 2 new hires to establish procedures for receiving staff information for corporate publications. Awarded 2 Recognition Awards in 2 years for shaping new unit.

Education: *Goldey Beacon College, Wilmington, DE*   **1991**
Classes in Administrative Office Management

Systems Skills: IBM, Lotus 1–2–3
Macintosh, Microsoft Word
Aldus PageMaker
DoveFax

William Sargent
12 Prospect Street
Providence, RI 02906
Tel: (401) 831–1164

Objective: Working in a retail or commercial sales group committed to high–growth efforts to gain market share and add substantial net profits.

Background Summary: Assigning goals and establishing territories for regional markets. Ensuring high market share through proven methods of cold calling and advertising efforts.

Retail Sales Experience:

Penobscot Retailers, Portland, ME   *1991*
Regional Sales Manager

- Coordinated $35,000 advertising test campaign through radio and newspaper markets. Produced 1200 leads for sales staff and netted 350 purchase orders. Returned over $100,000 in profit; realized 3:1 profit over expense margin.

- Set up computerized tracking program for blanketing areas with cold calling efforts. Monitored efforts of 25 sales people. Used 3–tier effort to gain client sale within 3 months. Realized 55% sales on initial visit, 30% at 6th–week follow–up and remaining 15% at end of 3–month term.

- Doubled yearly sales in 10 months.

Cleveland Sales Group, Pawtucket, RI   *1985–1990*
Sales Manager

- Planned market penetration for 6 New England states. Assigned territories for 15 sales people. Created monthly reporting system to track quota fulfillment and for determining sliding scale bonuses, paid by quarter.

- Increased sales by at least 30% per year over 5–year period. Moved from $1.8 million to $5.5 million in gross sales per year.

- Marketed products with focus on bottom–line profit margins. Reorganized product sales plans, increasing gross earnings from 28¢ to 40¢ per dollar.

- Undertook 2–year study to revamp product lines. Eliminated 8 trailing items and introduced 12 replacements. Added significant revenues(1.5+ million) to yearly gross earnings.

Education: **Western New England College, Springfield, MA**   *1985*
B.S., Marketing

Additional Achievements:
New England Medical Sales Award/Platinum Distinction   *1989*
New England Medical Sales Award/Gold Distinction   *1988*

Roberta Martin
8369 Melrose Place
Los Angeles, CA 90069
Tel: (213) 658–2649

Job Objective: Continuing highest standards of quality while delivering sought after analytical skills in a securities environment.

Qualified By: Demonstrating high–level knowledge of securities industry, using skills to analyze performance of field offices, restructure sales and support staff and develop long–term plans to gain market share.

Professional Background:

Delphi Brokerage, Inc., Los Angeles, CA   **1982–1991**
Senior Securities Analyst

- Accepted 6–month regional assignment to reorganize field office. Outfitted office with desktop computers on common network. Wrote plan for staff, raising yearly net profits by 35%. Completed assignment in 4 months.

- Specialized in analysis of all government securities. Produced introductory guides to each investment vehicle for new and existing clients. Used literature to promote changes in client portfolios. Increased sales by 60%.

- Wrote bi–weekly bulletins for clients with access to computers. Delivered timely recommendations via modem every other Friday at 4 p.m. for weekend review. Translated into increased activity Monday morning, averaging 75% in additional 1–day sales.

- Trained new analysts, averaging 5 per year, over 4–year period. Developed training program to include research, participation in client conferences and quarterly testing for 1 year. Gave results to personnel to assist in reviews and bonuses.

Rowe Group, Los Angeles, CA   **1977–1981**
Securities Analyst

- Acted as primary contact for active, high net–worth clients, via fax and modem transmissions. Participated in team effort to respond to requests. Reduced average response time from 2 business days to 6 hours.

- Prevented any interruptions to client service during reorganization and 25% reduction in staff. Coordinated efforts of remaining staff, increasing sales of recommended securities by 10% over previous year.

Education: **Pepperdine University**   **1972**
B.S., Business Administration

Memberships: **Securities Dealers Association**   **1977–1991**

141

Carl Tuttle
15 Chambers Street
Princeton, NJ 08540
Tel: (609) 924–0558

Objective: Working in an audit department for a growth–oriented corporation.

Summary of Qualifications: Using proven audit skills to ensure compliance to banking regulations. Managing training schedules to maintain high levels of expertise, offering senior management reliable measures of audit staff performance and reports denoting audit status of each product line.

Work Experience:

Princeton Bank, Princeton, NJ   1990–1991
Audit Manager

- Established centralized reporting function for audit staff. Bought 1 software application to allow for standardized reporting. Set up shared network of p.c.'s, with availability to various audit information determined by access code. Installed mechanism to prevent changing any documents.

- Managed training program for all audit and operations staff. Coordinated efforts of 2 trainers to conduct classes for 18 per month.

- Drafted control procedures for internal audit requirements. Received approval of plan to enact measures which saved $18,000 in audit department budget.

Boston Insurance, Boston, MA   1986–1989
Auditor

- Performed extensive audit on all Operations functions. Discovered discrepancies in reporting. Rewrote procedures for generating reports to senior management. Set up review committee to produce 1 monthly document versus previous submission of 6 separate reports. Cut 13 hours per month in management hours.

- Assisted manager of audit training in developing audit procedure manuals. Produced 4 manuals for reviewing Eastern and Western divisions, covering all variations in product lines.

Education: **Glassboro State College**   1986
B.S., Accounting

Systems Applications:

In–House, Trust Accounting System, Princeton Bank
In–House, Sales and Contract Systems, Boston Insurance
Macintosh Hardware
Microsoft Excel
IBM Hardware
Lotus 1–2–3

142

Jerry Murphy
565 East 65th Street
Indianapolis, IN 46220
Tel: (317) 255–4961

Objective: Automating processing for accounting groups, reducing processing hours and adding to company profits.

Summarized Qualifications: Transferring manual environments into more efficient, software–based operations. Managing change to automation, providing better quality of service, reducing man hours and costs through streamlined processing.

Work Background:

Scraggs & Munnis, Indianapolis, IN *1987–1991*
Senior Accountant

- Created, with 3 programmers, unique software for calculating bidding contracts. Included analysis of union costs, materials and any miscellaneous hard and soft dollar expenses. Calculated bids 9 days faster, on average, than previous method.

- Chose computer software for payroll processing for 35 union contract help. Reduced manual processing by 10 hours per week.

- Sent 2 trainers to seminars to learn new developments in accounting software. Authorized purchase of new software and supervised installation and training program for all accounting staff.

- Gained higher quality control through automated processing and reduced man hours by 35%, cutting staff by 4.

- Attended 3 regional workshops to focus on streamlining efforts particular to the construction industry. Enacted 10 recommendations over 3 years which saved $26,000+ in yearly office and site expense.

Perkins Elmwood & McGrath, Indianapolis, IN *1984–1986*
Accountant

- Introduced computer–based bookkeeping system, cutting staff by 2 and saving $50,000+ in salary and processing time.

- Prepared 3 core training manuals for company policies, citing controls for union costs, construction materials and allocations for all soft dollar expenses.

- Helped move 20 staff from affiliate offices to 1 centralized location.

Education: **Marian College** *1984*
B.S., Accounting

Janice Sheehan
260 William Street
Fredericksburg, VA 22401
Tel: (703) 371–2288

Job Objective: Winning foundation grants to introduce computers to all elementary grade levels.

Qualified By: Teaching students how to gain critical analytical and creative skills using computer technology. Writing grant proposals and getting corporate and foundation monies to buy computers and all supporting materials.

Professional Experience:

Fredericksburg Academy, Fredericksburg, VA   1986–1991
Elementary Teacher

- Applied for private grant to introduce computers at test site for 3rd grade students. Won approval and received $15,000.

- Purchased 4 computers and 2 printers, introduced training program for 1 year and won full acceptance of test project. Awarded additional $45,000 to further integrate program throughout all elementary levels.

- Established committee to inform parents, students and teachers of all needs of program. Worked with parents and school board to plan community and corporate fund drives. Raised $26,000. Set up separate board to determine allocation of funds.

- Taught grades 3 through 6. Met with parents 3 to 4 times per year. Created alternative measures of performance and set remedial training.

- Identified cultural, civic and political groups that would participate in student field trips. Took up to 5 field trips each year, all supported in part by funds provided by visited organization.

- Honored with Hope Blanshield Award for excellence in education. Accepted $7,500 award on behalf of Fredericksburg Academy.

Averett College, Danville, VA   1984–1985
Work Study Assignments

- Worked for Averett College admissions office. Developed skills using Macintosh equipment and numerous software applications. Bought and trained all staff on using fax modem, sending and receiving all fax transmissions via computer.

Education: *Averett College, Danville, VA*
M.S., Education   1986
B.S., Sociology; Minor in Elementary Education   1985

Additional Experience:

- Wrote, performed and co–directed 3 college plays. Won the Stephens Award, with $1,000 prize, for best amateur dramatic production.

```
                                                    Barbara Hammit
                                                5215 2nd Avenue South
                                                   Seattle, WA 98108
                                                 Tel: (206) 762–5126
```

Objective: Specializing in telecommunications sales to corporate clients.

**Summary of
Qualifications:**   *Signing contracts for medium–sized and start–up corporations,
adding significant and stable revenues to quarterly earnings.
Blanketing regional markets with cold calling and
lead advertising.*

Experience: **Data Communications, Inc., Seattle, WA**   *1988–1991*
Senior Sales Representative

- Achieved highest record of sales for consecutive 14–month
  period.

- Lead all field staff in signing new clients, ensuring company
  of an expanded and stable client base. Added 65 corporate
  accounts in 11 months.

- Set action plan for group of 5 sales representatives to blanket
  segmented markets each month. Created 2–step method of
  selling product; made cold calls with follow–up in–person
  meetings. Tracked calling with computer. Increased sales by
  20% per year.

- Met with research and development staff 1 to 2 times per quarter.
  Presented client "wish lists". Worked with R&D to address
  client concerns, making up to 5 product modifications each year.

- Resigned 93% of existing client base at contract term, maintaining
  highest resigning record in regional market.

Orion Digital Telecommunications, Inc., Spokane, WA   *1985–1987*
Analyst

- Participated in reorganization of 85–person office.
  Assigned responsibility for 12–member team, consolidating
  job functions and reassigning 3 staff to 3 other departments.

- Gained 6 new staff members through reorganization effort.
  Headed training program, getting new staff trained within
  8 months. Finished training in 5 months.

- Selected as 1 of 2 persons to receive corporate Achievement Award
  for excellence. Received extra vacation week and trip to New York.

Systems Skills: *Macintosh Hardware, Classic, SE30, II Family
Microsoft Word, Microsoft Excel*

Sheila Green
480 South Flagler Drive
West Palm Beach, FL 33401
Tel: (407) 659–7077

Job Objective: Reorganizing corporate offices to maximize productivity while controlling and minimizing costs.

Summarized
Qualifications: Reviewing corporate objectives and installing long–range directives which meet and exceed expectations. Analyzing service needs, then reducing personnel costs by replacing some permanent staff with short–term contract help.

Professional
Background: **Wagner Technical Consultants, Palm Beach, FL**   *1985–1991*
Senior Manager, Office Support

- Advanced a new reorganization plan to cut permanent staff by 10%. Received approval from executive office, enacting changes which reduced staff by 22 and saved $500,000+ in payroll expense.

- Contracted with temporary placement services for most word processing functions. Kept 2 staff members for all immediate senior management assignments; replaced 15 people with on–call workers. Saved $60,000.

- Offered plan for replaced workers to become independent contractors, with 11 of 15 accepting. Increased net pay to workers while reducing overall personnel expense substantially.

- Worked out plan with personnel manager to introduce multiple health plan selections. Went from 1 to 3 plans offered; allocated extra expenses to staff, adding no additional costs to corporation.

- Managed salary review process for 30 staff. Created 3–step method for performance evaluation. Prepared, with each staff member, yearly objectives, 6–month oral and written analyses and 1 year final review and pay raise.

Parson Mumford Partners, Atlanta, GA   *1980–1984*
Manager, Training & Development

- Managed training and development staff of 9. Met with departmental heads to determine upcoming needs of various product lines. Wrote itineraries for 3–month period, informing all staff with electronic mail and follow–up newsletter.

- Taught 2 classes per quarter. Developed objectives with 9 trainers, attended at least one session per trainer, per quarter, to assure adherence to corporate training methodology.

Education: **Texas A&M University**   *1980*
B.A., English

Wayne Green
254 Hamilton Row
Birmingham, MI 48009
Tel: (313) 540–2994

Objective: Providing technical expertise in programming for medium
and large–sized corporations.

Qualified by: Leading banking, investment and engineering groups to greater
efficiencies by streamlining management and "backshop" processing.

**Professional
Background:**

Barker Temporary Agency, Birmingham, MI 1990–1991
Computer Analyst

- Planned and performed all aspects of systems analysis, design
  and development for investment management performance tool.
  Oversaw 3 programmers implement specifications. Finished
  2.5 months ahead of schedule and $16,000 under budget.

- Maintained 200 technical files for engineering office. Referenced
  files by staff number, job specification and completion status.

- Set up method for President to print weekly status reports on all
  completed, in–progress and out–for–bid jobs.

Wayne Green, Inc., Detroit, MI 1979–1989
Independent Assignments

- Tested quality assurance programs to assure conformance with
  senior management directives. Discovered 2 programming errors
  in contract software which gave incorrect results in 35% of cases.
  Made corrections, saving $40,000 in unnecessary expenditures.

- Coordinated programming changes to banking data center.
  Changed batch transmissions, rescheduled report packaging and
  recycled night processing. Cut 1.5 hours off end–of–day processing,
  allowing for staff access to system at 7 a.m. versus 8:30 a.m..

- Assisted Project Director implement 2–year conversion project.
  Helped form business plans, report on budgets and establish
  achievable goals. Prepared monthly reports showing monthly
  expenditures of $80,000.

- Handled 15 separate assignments over 10 year period.

**Systems
Skills:** IBM mainframes: COBOL, OS/JCL and MVS.
Working knowledge of CICS and IDMS.

Education: **Boston University, Boston, MA** 1984–1990
B.S., Computer Science

147

Thomas Brewster
36 Main Street
Cincinnati, OH 45243
Tel: (513) 561–6814

Job Objective: *Negotiating commercial space for large corporate clients.*

**Summary of
Qualifications:** Analyzing client needs, determining best usage of space and arranging long–term contracts. Selling properties held both independently and in–house.

Background: *Parker Management Company, Cincinnati, OH*   1988–1991
Broker

- Renegotiated lease arrangement with major corporation. Changed terms of lease, adding $7 per square foot. Raised lease payments by $100,000+ per year.

- Finalized 3–year deal with high–priority client, lowering flat rates but adding percentage earnings based on client gross revenues. Added $370,000 to earnings due to amendment in deal.

- Represented company interests on 60 in–house properties. Oversaw accounting functions and maintenance contracts. Worked with 7 various contract staff to maintain buildings and gain community honors.

- Honored with Cincinnati Community Stewardship Award for distinguished commitment to 3 area neighborhoods.

Harbor Real Estate, Boston, MA   1985–1987
Broker

- Won exclusive 2–year contract for brokering space for 2 major downtown Boston developers. Agreed to quarterly sales quotas for 16 properties. Met requirements for each quarter and extended contract for additional 2 years.

- Prepared quarterly figures for accountants for all tax reporting, filing state and federal reports according to government schedules.

- Increased gross earnings by $200,000 in 10–month period.

- Processed payroll for 12 agents on weekly basis.

Education: *Marietta College*   1984
B.A., Philosophy

Memberships: *Cincinnati Brokers Group*
Cincinnati Partners(Board Member)
National Realtors Association
Greater Boston Real Estate Brokers Association

Anne Powers
5300 Roswell Road
Atlanta, GA 30342
Tel: (404) 250–6637

Objective: Supporting the office support needs of a medical staff in a cooperative, private practice environment.

Qualified By: Using knowledge of medial office practices and office systems to assist doctors and nurses in providing the best, most expedient care to patients. Automating files, introducing computers and handling support tasks to generate highest industry rankings in client service.

Experience: **Atlanta Medical Group, Atlanta, GA** 1988–1991
Medical Assistant/Office Manager

- Outfitted office with new telecommunications system, allowing for patient selection and automatic transfer of calls to appropriate offices. Reduced general calls by 200+ and cut 14 staff hours per week.

- Installed 18 computers using same network. Gave doctors and nurses immediate access to patient files. Reduced data retrieval costs by arranging licensing agreement with software company providing system. Increased active patients per staff by 20%.

- Prepared data for medical staff. Used software to retrieve and print patient histories for 15 doctors and nurses. Transferred all client files to database. Eliminated 300 square feet of storage space.

- Interpreted computerized test results for patients. Created charts which gave common terms to medical language. Met with affiliate organizations to introduce similar interpretation charts.

- Assisted in patient tests and analysis of results to learn of any methods of computer–aided efficiencies.

Safeguard Partnership, Atlanta, GA 1985–1987
Assistant Office Manager

- Researched laboratory equipment companies for directors. Presented findings which resulted in $80,000 in purchases decisions.

- Helped office manager set up a standardized 3–week training program for new hires. Wrote 2 parts of a 5–part manual which covered all aspects of supporting medical staff.

- Trained all new hires and supported all staff on in–house data retrieval system. Worked with programmers 1 or 2 times per year to introduce modifications.

Education: **Atlanta State University** 1986–1988
Courses in Business Administration

149

Your Cover Letters

A cover letter is your best opportunity to slant your credentials towards a specific prospect. Here's why:

1. You'll address, point by point, how you qualify for the job. You'll have reviewed a written or oral job description or newspaper advertisement. Your cover letter will meet every known qualification required, or make up for them with equally valuable skills.

2. You'll show that you can write effectively.

3. You'll show the employer that you can communicate on their level. You'll demonstrate that your level of expertise matches their level of need.

4. You'll make the reader want to read the résumé. The employer will want to have the opportunity of meeting you.

Through your whole job search, and especially the writing of cover letters, you must accept all responsibilities for your success. The cover letter is brief, clear and powerful. You'll allow for no guesswork on the part of the employer. The employer is not going to guess that you're skilled, suppose you're talented, assume you can write or hope you're the person for the job.

You'll make the employer understand that you are the right and only choice.

"I make my own success."

Say this sentence aloud three times and with conviction every day.

"I make my own success."
"I make my own success."
"I make my own success."

Post that sentence on the refrigerator or on a bedside table. Repeat it every day. Repeat it before going to sleep. That sentence personalizes the search. That sentence gives you four things:

1. The 'I' and 'my' are the greatest self–identifiers.
2. The word 'make' suggests action and creation.
3. The word 'own' suggests tangible property that belongs to you.
4. 'Success' is a positive suggestion of all those qualifications that make your life better.

There are rules for you to follow when writing your cover letter. While exceptions to everything in life do exist, follow these rules. They are:

1. Keep the cover letter to one page only. You've learned that short, powerful statements work on your résumé. Likewise, a short and direct statement of qualifications directed toward a specific employer will work on your cover letter.

2. Spell everything correctly. This includes name and address of recipient, as well as the whole content of the letter.

3. Keep the cover letter to four paragraphs, if possible. The first paragraph will be your introduction. The second and third will highlight qualifications. The fourth will be a closing statement that suggests a next step to be taken.

4. The cover letter must be typed or entered into a word processor. If typed, absolutely no correction fluids or smudges are allowed.

5. Use a good quality bond paper. Personal stationery is acceptable only if graphics are not included. No cats, no paw prints, no flowers, etc.. The employer may be biased against your personal interests.

6. Format should be clean and easy to read. I suggest a 2–inch border at the top and bottom margins of the page and a 1 1/2–inch border for the left and right margins.

Just so we're sure you understand the most important rule, repeat after me. "I will never use a 2(or more)–page cover letter." Thank you.

The purpose of the cover letter is not to repeat your résumé. Rather, the cover letter highlights those skills and achievements that best benefit a prospective employer. And, the cover letter makes the reader anxious to learn more (the résumé). We've said this at the beginning of the chapter and now we'll say it again. Repeat it as many times as needed until you understand the difference between the cover letter and the résumé. You want to give more. You don't want to repeat your message.

Special Note on Using Names in Your Cover Letter

First, use them whenever possible. Use them in the salutation and in the content. Consider your own mail. You probably give more attention to letters addressed to you than to those marked 'occupant'. When you include names, observe the following:

1. Names are correctly and fully written. Never abbreviate.

2. Use accurate titles. Never abbreviate.

3. If someone has recommended you for the position, follow steps 1 and 2 above. Include the persons name who has recommended you in the first paragraph of your cover letter. Note their relationship to the employer, if possible. For example:

Dear Mr. Smith:

Mrs. Sylvia Johnson, Vice President in charge of marketing at the Johnson Company, suggested I contact you regarding your open position for Marketing Analyst. My qualifications fully meet the...

4. If you are replying to an advertisement, in whatever media, identify that media and the job title. Don't assume the recipient will know which position your material corresponds to. For example:

"I am responding to your advertisement in the Manchester Tribune for a Systems Analyst. As my résumé proves, I will contribute to each of your needs.

My qualifications fully..."

The cover letter should hit them hard with a personalized reason for them to meet you. Your cover letter will get them to read the résumé. Both together get you the meeting. All three will get you the job.

Do not use any negative language or criticisms of any kind. Don't put down other companies or products to sell your argument. If you do, the employer will assume that you wouldn't hesitate to put them down in the future.

Ask for a meeting. Ask for an interview. Let them know what you want. If you are only looking for information, say so. Don't let them assume anything. If you are not clear in purpose, the reader may try to figure you out or trash the letter. Whatever you do, don't let your intentions be misconstrued for the worse.

You may apply for a job through personal references, networking contacts, advertisements and so forth. In every case, your cover letter should address each and every qualification outlined in the job description. You may even determine an advantage if you repeat the ad word for word in the summary of qualifications in your cover letter.

We'll look at five ads and the resulting cover letters. Compare what is asked for with what is offered. (Note: The addresses, dates, salutations and sign–offs of the cover letters have been left out of the examples. What remains is the "meat" of the letter.)

1st Advertisement:

Marketing/Sales Manager
A recent opening has been created for a marketing/sales manager. This job reports directly to the Div. Exec. and will develop sales strategies as well as presentations. Qualified candidates will have selling and marketing skills in a securities–related field. Must be able to work independently. Send your credentials as well as salary history to: Bob Carlsen, Howard Industries, 1 Main Street, Newton, MA, 02195.

Cover Letter:

I am responding to your advertisement in The Boston Globe for a Marketing/Sales Manager.

For 5 years, I have been reporting directly to a Division Executive. I have been responsible for developing sales strategies and presenting them to banking and investment environments. I am able to work independently and have reported to straightline as well as matrix management.

I have also worked for Mr. David Mauder, who has held one of the marketing/sales management positions at your firm. I'm sure Mr. Mauder would confirm the credentials shown on my résumé as well as my ability to excel in this position.

I will call you on Tuesday to set up an appointment.

2nd Advertisement:

Social Worker
Position to provide case management, home visitations, intake evaluations and developing parent support service network. Must have experience with young children and families and be LCSW with knowledge of early childhood/special education. Send résumé and salary history to Ellen M. Greenwood, Farber Health Center, Personnel Office, 55 Prospect Street, Ridgefield, CT, 06877.

Cover Letter:

I am responding to the internal job posting for a social worker position at Farber Health Center.

I am fully qualified to provide case management, home visitations and intake evaluations. At DeWitt Counseling, I have developed parent support service networks, focusing on both pre–school and familial situations. I have managed a program dealing with physically disabled children and am LCSW.

The enclosed résumé highlights proven abilities and experience. Farber Health Center maintains highest industry standards, the same standards I maintain in my professional life. I'm sure I would prove a valuable asset to your firm.

I will call you this Friday to set up a mutually convenient appointment.

3rd Advertisement:

Programmer/Analyst
Interested candidates will develop all specifications for our customer service division. You should have 3+ years experience of proven programming skills with expertise in COBOL and "C" as well as an ability to work with senior management. BA/BS essential. Respond to: Powers Group, Jeremy Rober, Code K–1, 213 Fairview Road, Bethesda, MD, 20014.

Cover Letter:

Mr. Timothy Barns, Senior Analyst at Powers Group, suggested I present my qualifications for your available position as Programmer/Analyst.

For 2 years I have developed all specifications for the customer service division of Anthony Development Group. I have 5+ years experience of proven programming skills with knowledge of 4 languages, with particular expertise in COBOL.

I have reported directly to senior management teams on a variety of projects. I'm able to work well with every level of staff and management.

As the enclosed résumé shows, my experience and education would be of great benefit to your firm. I'm very proud of my education at Boston University, earning a B.S. in Computer Sciences and maintaining a 3.8 average. Coupled with 3 years of proven work experience, I have much to offer a dynamic and growing firm such as the Powers Group.

I will call you on Wednesday of next week to set up an appointment.

4th Advertisement:

Bookkeeper
Bookkeeper wanted. A part–time job, 30 hours, experienced in bookkeeping practices. Knowledge of federal contracts helpful. Send résumé to Ames Contracting, Attn: Kathleen Ohn, 150 Franklin St., Chatham, NY, 12037.

Cover Letter:

I am responding to your advertisement in the Chatham Courier for the position of Bookkeeper.

As my résumé shows, I have considerable experience in bookkeeping practices. I am familar with a wide variety of contracts, particularly those that affect the contracting business.

I'm quite flexible in the hours that I am able to work and am available to work a 30–hour week. I'm sure that the skills I'd bring to your firm would prove to be a valuable asset.

I will be in Chatham on Thursday of next week. I will call you on Monday to arrange for a mutually convenient time for us to meet.

5th Advertisement:

Vice President/Retail Management
We are seeking a strong retail exec. who can manage existing products while developing new markets. The requirements include understanding development disciplines, strategic planning and 8+ years as a senior exec. in retail. Familiarity with computer technologies is helpful. Interested candidates should send résumé, cover letter and salary requirements to GGB Confidential, Dept H–4, 10 Harrison Ave., Chicago, IL, 60611.

Cover Letter

I am responding to your advertisement in the Wall Street Journal for the position of Vice President/Retail Management.

I have 12+ years experience as a senior executive in retail management. The enclosed résumé highlights proven skills in the apparel, appliance and service industries. While managing existing product lines which have contributed $100+ million to gross revenues, I have chaired various committees responsible for introducing new and existing products to new markets.

I am also familiar with both IBM and DEC mainframe environments. My computer experience, detailed on my résumé, includes both training and programming.

I would appreciate your calling me either Tuesday or Thursday of next week, between 4:30 and 7 p.m., at my home telephone. I look forward to your call.

Meet and excel at all the qualifications asked for and you've significantly increased your chances for an interview. Ignore their needs and they'll ignore you.

What if you don't have all the skills required? First, don't assume you are out of the running. Simply overcompensate with other qualifications. If you don't have a college degree, show the extensive experience and training you do have that more than makes up for the missing diploma. If you don't know their computer language, show how easy it was for you to learn four other languages and how quickly you would learn a fifth.

Quick Tip

Did you notice that in every instance we did not give out the requested salary information? You should by now understand why. Yes? Do not get yourself screened out of the process due to salary incompatibility. You are certainly talented enough to structure compensation to your benefit at a later date. If you do give a salary figure and your qualifications meet their needs, you do not want a telephone call stating "You're hired. Start Monday at 8:30". (Trust us, this is true. You'll have met all their conditions, but how do you know they'll meet any of yours?)

Make them understand that hiring you will only add to their success.

Your References

References may be critically important to you. Some employers will call every reference given and question them in detail. Others will ignore a reference list altogether.

You should remember that your references may include anyone of your choosing. While other books may, for example, suggest excluding a family member or pastor, you should decide who best will help your cause. Still, if you have three or four references on your list, you should include at least two people who are not related and who worked with you in a professional capacity.

When asked, you should provide the interviewer with a printed list of your references. Each reference will include the following:

1. Full name. Title, if helpful to your case.
2. Address, as preferred by the reference.
3. Telephone number.
4. Professional or personal relationship.

Include your own name, address and telephone number on the sheet as well. Name the sheet 'References'. Consider the example on the following page:

Janice Smithson
16 East 57th Street
New York, NY 10022
Tel: (212) 753–1492

References:

David Jacobs
148 Lexington Avenue at 30th Street
New York, NY 10016
Telephone: (212) 683–3156
Relationship: Manager, XYZ Corporation

Francis Petersham
2816 Pennsylvania Avenue, NW
Washington, DC 20007
Telephone: (202) 965–2273
Relationship: Associate, XYZ Corporation

Cleveland Bricher
10 East 70th Street
New York, NY 10021
Telephone: (212) 744–4862
Relationship: Division Executive, EFG, Inc.

Susan Babson
719 Fifth Avenue
New York, NY 10019
Telephone: (212) 767–3155
Relationship: Personal Reference

Other books may suggest that the material just presented should be enough information regarding references. As with every other part of this book, we want you to be wholly prepared. We want to address those subjects that even writers of career self–help books don't like to explore in depth. Let's go that next step with the following statement:

"References, even close friends and acquaintances, may actually hurt more than help my job campaign."

Remember this important statement when deciding whom to present as a reference. References might hurt you in so many ways, intentionally or unintentionally. Choosing a reference will come after asking yourself many questions. For instance, does the reference:

1. Know that he or she is a reference?

Will the reference:

1. Speak clearly and effectively?
2 Have a brash or arrogant telephone manner, or one that is direct and pleasant?
3. Know what type of job you are looking for?
4. Look forward to fighting for your cause?

Looking back at your relationship, will the reference:

1. Remember how late you stayed for four months to get the project finished on schedule? Do they remember it was <u>four months,</u> especially since it occurred 5 years ago?
2. Hold any type of grudge? Did other bosses like you better than any others? Will the reference use this against you?
3. Think you advanced faster than you should have?
4. Try to sell their own skills to the employer?
5. Disagree with any part of the interviewers' assessment of you?

Will you be able to prevent the reference from:

1. Giving away your past salary history?

2. Exposing any weaknesses you have?
3. Badmouthing your previous employer?

A reference has to have your best interests at heart. You must let them know what your best interests are.

You've got to let every reference know what it is you are doing, how you plan to achieve what you are setting out to do and how they may help you. You might accomplish this in person, via telephone or through the mail. Whatever method you follow, the reference must receive the same information on paper.

If you visit a reference or call them, will they remember all the points you made? What if you visited them two months ago? Will they still remember? After each promising interview, you will contact them, address key points they should remember and ask them to review the written material left with them earlier.

Have extra copies of what you've given to them. They may lose the originals. Deliver everything to them by hand if possible. Fax the material or mail it via overnight delivery. Whatever you do, ensure that they have all appropriate information before they receive that telephone call from the interviewer.

What should the reference have? I suggest three things:

1. A cover letter addressed to them.
2. A summary of the specific contributions you'll make to the employer. You may decide to include this summary in the cover letter or on a separate piece of paper.
3. Your résumé.

If you've told the truth throughout your campaign, you'll find no problem in giving them this information. You may have instances, however, where you have changed company terminology to better fit a wider job market. A 'Designer for Internal Applications, Grade 5' may have been changed to

'Systems Analyst'. Explain any changes made in your cover letter to the reference.

A very important point for you to remember is that a cover letter to a reference should tell them exactly what not to say. If you are progressing in your career, and you've decided to stress some skills over others, tell the reference what you intend to do and ask for them to highlight only the skills you want to take to the new employer. If you specify what help you are looking for, most references will be more than willing to oblige you.

A summary of specific contributions basically tells the reference what to say. The interviewers' questions will be answered, but the reference will be coached in their responses. The reference can add so much more to the conversation, all based on your direction.

If the interviewer asks for any various additional comments from the reference, the reference will be prepared with the information you've supplied. They'll be able to add all those additional contributions you've identified.

The résumé provides the reference with the dates you worked at various jobs and the titles you'd prefer to use to better fit your market search. Of course, the cover letter and the résumé provided to the reference may open new opportunities for you. Since the reference will clearly and completely understand what you want, you may find additional job leads coming your way.

You'll need a separate cover letter and summary of specific qualifications for each reference. You'll want them to highlight your achievements with them, not with your whole career. There is good reason for this approach.

Sending the same cover letter and summary of specific qualifications to all references may hurt you. If the interviewer calls each reference and they all answer with the same stock answers, watch out. The interviewer will worry about the integrity of the references and the appropriateness of hiring you.

We'll look at the material sent to two references. Review the résumé and read how each reference is approached differently. You'll understand how each reference is shown how they may contribute individually to the interviewer. Good luck!

Mary A. Parsons
20 Pinckney Street, No. 3
Boston, MA 02114
Tel: (617) 523–0135

Objective: Working with high net–worth clients in a banking environment.

Summary of Qualifications: Managing all transactions for large accounts, affecting both cash and securities. Using solid industry knowledge to handle all client concerns, gaining both client confidence and additional accounts.

Professional Background:

Prime Bank, Boston, MA   1987–1991
Senior Account Officer, Institutional Custody   1989–1991

- Managed 100 accounts, including endowments, pensions and operating accounts with total value of $2.5+ billion. Acted as primary contact to prestigious area universities and foundations, generating $700,000+ in annual fees.

- Researched and resolved highly sensitive issues related to restricted securities. Expedited transfer of donor gifts to $1 billion fund drive.

- Troubleshot foreign trade problems, working with foreign securities agencies to reclaim fund discrepancies. Returned $85,000 to department.

Account Officer, Institutional Custody   1987–1988

- Administered 40 accounts valued at $1 billion, realizing $250,000+ in fees.

- Coordinated account concerns between clients, investment managers, brokers and affiliate departments. Settled trades(150+ per week), solved cash balance problems and resolved share discrepancies.

- Represented department as division converted to ABC, a service bureau trust accounting system. Oversaw data integrity project, updating system files in preparation of $50+ billion conversion.

Partner Savings Bank, Dallas, TX   1986–1987
Loan Accountant, Accounting Division

- Handled accounting for all loans in mortgage subsidiary portfolio. Calculated overnight investments.

Education: **University of Michigan**   1986
B.B.A., Finance and Managerial Economics

Achievements:
- Received Prime Bank award for outstanding achievement in developing user manual and training test–site clients on ABC Trust System.

- Volunteered as tutor for Massachusetts Campaign for Literacy.

Reference A

Your Address

Date

Mr. Chad Berenson
Senior Analyst
Partner Savings Bank
15 Thompson Street
Dallas, TX 75205

Dear Chad:

I was very pleased to speak with you recently. As I mentioned, I am planning a job search and appreciate using your name as a reference.

I plan to work for a large marketing firm, analyzing products and producing cost estimations. While I served as a loan accountant when working for you, I would like to stress the details of the overnight transactions I handled.

For my new position, I would like the employer to understand how critical accurate calculations were to the company. I'd also appreciate it if you'd show the employer that errors on my part would have caused substantial losses if they had happened.

I've included my résumé for your reference. Chad, I'm really glad I can count on your help. Best regards to you.

Sincerely,

Mary Parsons

Enclosure

Reference B

Your Address

Date

Mrs. Susan Brown
Vice President
Prime Bank
10 Temple Place
Boston, MA 02110

Dear Mrs. Brown:

It was a pleasure speaking with you on Tuesday. I know your schedule is very full and I appreciate the time you took out of your day for our conversation.

As I move on in a new career direction, the value of you as a reference would benefit me as I transfer my skills to a new field. I am researching and plan to work for a large marketing firm. Many of the demands of this field have a correlation with the banking business. In summary, I want to show the following:

1. An ability to handled large, critical transactions daily.
2. Proven experience as a project leader, evaluating products and having the ability to work with programming staff.
3. A track record of working throughout all levels of management and with the most sensitive accounts.
4. A commitment to earn and save money for the company, with the particular goal of uncovering lost fees.

You'll also note that the enclosed résumé lists my last position with Prime Bank as Senior Account Officer. I know that our official term was Senior Leader Grade 14. I have changed the title to a more generic title that applies to a wider audience.

Thank you so much for your willingness to participate in my career growth plans. I'll be in touch as I move to realize my plans.

Best regards,

Mary Parsons

Enclosure

Preparing for the Interview

You'll win if you are prepared. Period.

You've done so much to prepare for your interview. If you think of some missed detail during the interview itself, you're bound to become somewhat tense. Pay attention to details. Details pay off. Do you realize that many people hire candidates based on appearance, going after a certain 'look'? If 8 apply for a job and 4 have a less than polished appearance, you've possibly doubled your chances of getting the job. Of course, you are not one of the four that were eliminated. Correct?

Following is a checklist of items for men and women both. Then, separate checklists are provided for each sex. The items on these checklists all relate to your presentation and appearance during the interview process.

For Men and Women   **Yes**   **No**

Do you have:

1. At least 6 copies of your résumé?
2. Your research for that particular interview?
3. Your summary of qualifications for the interview?
4. A list of questions you'll want to ask, if needed?
5. Your transportation arrangements?
   a. Do you have your bus or train schedule?
   b. Have you performed a 'dry run' of the route?
   c. If possible, have you purchased your ticket?
6. Do you know where the meeting will take place?
   a. Do you have the address with you?

    b. Do you have the telephone number of your contact?

    c. Do you have the names of those you'll be seeing?

7. Are you wearing your watch?
   (If you don't own one, buy one.)
8. Do you have 2 or more pens and pencils, either full of ink or with sharpened tip?
9. Have you got enough cash on hand?

Is that everything? No, it isn't. Don't forget these:

1. Do you have a good, undamaged umbrella?
2. A good–looking pocket calendar?
3. A needle and thread in case of last–minute repairs?
4. Hair that is styled conservatively?
5. Fragrance that is subtle? (Or none at all. Period.)
6. A clean–shaven look(face for men, face and legs for women)?
7. A carrying folder, leather only, brown or tan, with no scratches, rips or badly aged bruises?

For Men   **Yes No**

If appropriate:

1. Is your suit or clothing pressed?
   (If you don't know how to iron, take your clothes to the dry cleaners. Wear freshly cleaned clothing to every interview. Never wear frayed clothing(collars, etc.).
2. Are your shoes well-polished, leather only and matching your carrying folder?
3. Is your belt free of scratches, leather only and matching your shoes?
4. Are you wearing a solid white or blue shirt?
   (Those are your only choices.)
5. Are you wearing a good, 100% silk tie, conservative in appearance? (No bow ties allowed.)
6. Are you sure that your socks will not allow your legs to be exposed, even when crossing your legs?
7. Is your jewelry modest? (You may wear a wedding band, signet ring and a watch. That's it. Absolutely no exposed neck chains, wrist bracelets or tie pins.)

8. Are you carrying a cotton or silk handkerchief?
   (You should not wear it in your outer jacket pocket.)

For Women   **Yes   No**

If appropriate:

1. A suit or dress that is pressed? (Your clothing
   should be natural fibers only. Also, you may wear
   a broader range of colors. Still, be conservative
   and subtle in expressing yourself.)

2. A strong pair of leather shoes, with no more than
   two–inch heels?

3. At least one extra pair of pantyhose?

4. You may wear jewelry. Be careful of your choices.
   Very simple, classic earrings are appropriate. If you
   want to wear bracelets, wear only one. Avoid jewelry
   which will cause noise distractions. A wedding ring
   or one other conservative ring is fine. Multiple rings,
   or rings on every finger is completely inappropriate
   for the interview.

5. If you wear a belt, the belt should be made of leather
   and match your shoes.

6. Makeup may be worn. Makeup should look natural.
   Period.

Remember, quality sells.

You would be wise to fill out the worksheet below a couple
days before each scheduled interview. This worksheet will help
your mind visualize the interview from start to finish. It need
only be general in terms. You simply want to walk through the
whole process and make sure you're covered in every area.

The Company

1. Their introduction:

_____

_____

_____

You

1. Your introduction:

_____

_____

_____

The Company

2. Their needs:

_____

_____

_____

_____

You

2. What you can contribute:

_____

_____

_____

_____

The Company

3. Your qualifications:

_____

_____

You

3. Your qualifications:

_____
_____
_____
_____

The Company

4. Their questions:

_____
_____
_____
_____
_____

You

4. Your questions:

_____
_____
_____
_____
_____

The Company

5. How they'll approach the next step(the job offer or the next interview):

_____
_____
_____

5. How you'll approach the next step(the job offer or the next interview:

_____

_____

_____

The Company

6. Closing remarks:

_____

_____

You

6. Closing remarks:

_____

_____

Items two and three in each section above are the real heart of the interview. Everything else supports them.

You may feel tense before the interview. The interview is not a common occurrence. Visualize the experience. Think of what the position is, where you'll be located during the interview and how you'll look when you accept the job. Treat yourself to a personal or job related gift. Buy yourself a great tie for that downtown banking job. A new cashmere sweater for the advertising agency. Any accessory, a bracelet, a leather bag, a classic pen or a new self–help book may give you the boost you want.

Another way to handle tense feelings is to create and maintain a support network. The network may only be one individual such as a spouse. This support may be too subjective to help you. For an objective partner or group, look to previous work mates or a removed professional relationship. The network might include a pastor, a fellow mason, a social club friend, etc..

Getting people to sign on allows for great possibilities of role–playing. Since you've just filled out worksheets from your perspective as well as the company perspective, you will be able to provide the necessary details for your network.

Make two copies of all the worksheets throughout the book. Explain your research to your trusted network. Tell the participants why you want to work in the industry or company you've chosen. Establish a dialog with the group and simulate as best as possible the conditions you'll face in the interview. Ask each role–player to be tough! You can always handle a tough situation if you have orchestrated it.

Quick Tip

Sometimes, it is difficult to decide whether or not to send a résumé in response to an advertisement. We suggest if you are interested in or qualified for half of the characteristics of the job you should send in the résumé. Does this make sense? Yes.

First, job descriptions are not necessarily written by the person managing the position. This means skills you may not have may not play an important role in the position. Second, the manager may have reanalyzed her needs and redefined the position. You may actually have 100% of the qualifications needed. Next, the position may be new. Through your research and during the interview, you may define the best job for you and for the company. Finally, the job description may be correct. During the interview, you may agree that you are not qualified for that particular position, yet another position may be available that you'd be great for. The interviewer will consider you to be perfect for the company and make a fit. Needed job skills may be better defined and you may decide to pursue them.

Visualize your entrance for the interview. Watch yourself display those characteristics most impressive to the interviewer:

1. Your genuine smile.
2. Your warm greeting.
3. Your projection of honesty and enthusiasm.
4. Your interest in the position.

5. Your positive attitude.

The interviewer is interested in selling the job to the *perceived* best prospect. Whether or not you're the best candidate, you'll get the job if the interviewer thinks you're the best candidate. This is an extremely critical point for you to understand.

You may actually be ranked 4th on the list in terms of skills. Yet, your presentation may rank you 1st and thus land the job. But, any time your attitude reveals thinking that you're not the best candidate for the job you'll lessen your chances of success. The interview is not the time to become internally or externally self-critical. Whether you think you are 1st or 85th, sell yourself as #1. Of course, you are welcome to sell yourself as better than #1!

We'll analyze the five characteristics above from the interviewers' perspective. You may give less importance to some of these characteristics. Hopefully we'll convince you to think otherwise.

Your genuine smile. Your warm greeting.

The importance of these qualities is obvious(or should be). A smile suggests friendliness. You'll suggest an ability to work with managers and subordinates. Your friendliness may help make sales when you warmly greet clients. Your smile shows you have good teeth and therefore good personal habits.

Your projection of honesty and enthusiasm.

First, honesty. If you lie on your résumé or application you'll have to support those lies at every moment in the future. Expected and unexpected moments. Your memory will always demonstrate and support past truths. The hesitancy in your voice, a slight stutter or a cold sweat will give away a lie or suggest hidden and undesirable qualities.

Your interest in the position.

The interviewer wants to know how much training you'll require. The interviewer will often supply the training if he senses you are genuinely interested in the job. On the other hand, if you might be a possible burden you'll soon be disqualified. A burden is someone who cooperates unwillingly.

Show you've researched the company, the department, the products and the goals of the company. Prove that you won't put a strain on those already employed. Project your contributions.

Answer "I don't know" to basic questions and you'll be in trouble. You certainly may ask for clarification. You may ask for specific details so that your answer will be better focused. Your answers may be broad or narrow in scope, but show your interest with examples of your research.

Your positive attitude.

A positive attitude suggests equality. You are not intimidated by the interviewer. You don't give the interviewer a subservient role in the search process. You're not arrogant or shy. Instead, with a positive attitude you've shown you are a team player. Dependable, interested in the success of the company and confident of your ability to make contributions.

The whole point of this chapter is to highlight your need to be prepared. Review these steps you should take the morning of or an hour before your interview. You should:

1. Make sure your wardrobe is spotless.
2. Have backup clothes that are clean and pressed.
3. Read a recap about the company you are going to see.
4. Reread your résumé.
5. Reread your cover letter.
6. Make sure you know the name and title of the interviewer.
7. Review interview questions that seem most important to the interview.

8. Breath deeply. Express your emotions. By whatever method, get your anxieties out of your system. Stretch or meditate. Arrive at an internal calmness.

Some things may be done in the privacy of your own home. Some things should never be done at an interview. Follow these rules:

1. Don't chew gum.
2. Don't bit your fingernails.
3. Don't file your fingernails.
4. Don't pick your teeth.
5. Don't pick your nose.
6. Don't scratch improperly.
7. Don't cover your mouth when speaking.
8. Don't wear sunglasses.

Many of these things may be done well before the interview(filing fingernails and cleaning teeth). Others may be done in a bathroom(scratching an itch). Perhaps other habits might be given up completely.

The most important don't

1. Don't be late.

If you are late, you've shown disregard and disrespect for the interviewers' time. You've shown that you don't care about giving yourself all the time allocated for you to give a full presentation. You may suggest that you won't be on time with clients. Maybe you'll arrive late for work each morning. Are you really able to handle the best assignments or should they be given to somebody else?

Avoid all of these negative thoughts. Be on time.

Quick Tip

If you plan more than two interviews each day you'll probably find yourself in a troubling spot very quickly. You may estimate how long an interview will last. At best, your prediction may be somewhat accurate. At worst, the first interview may last all day and jeopardize your chances at the other three interviews you scheduled that same day.

Here is a simple solution. Schedule one meeting in the morning, perhaps around 9 a.m. or 10 a.m.. Schedule another in the afternoon, either at 1 p.m. or at 2 p.m.. You'll give yourself a minimum of three hours between interviews. In rare instances you'll still have to cancel the afternoon meeting. Most likely, the morning interview will break as hunger sets in(for the interviewer). But again, be prepared. The interviewer may send you on to the next round of talks as she makes her way to lunch.

Always have the names and telephone numbers of everyone you'll see on a particular day. You may be far from home when you discover you need to contact an employer to change an appointment. The employer has no responsibility for your schedule, but will expect every consideration.

Avoid all negative possibilities. Be on time. And be prepared.

What to Look for During the Interview

You'll be able to develop skills to sense how you're doing at the interview. Certain signals will suggest whether or not the interviewer is interested in you. The interview is successful when:

1. The interviewer is genuinely impressed with your research.
2. You're told about an actual situation occurring at the company and asked how you would handle it.
3. They want to show you around the office and introduce you to some of your future co-workers.
4. They spend considerable time with you, going beyond the normal time allocation for the interview.
5. They ask you if you would talk with others about the job.
6. They discuss your salary requirements. The discussion of salary is more than wanting a figure from you. Don't give away information(an actual dollar figure).

7. They seem to be telling you why you should want to work for their company.

Preparing for the Salary Discussions

The interviewer may bring up salary requirements at any of three periods of the interview. Talk of salary can come early on, at the middle or end of the interview. You may be asked for your salary history, the exact dollar figure you are earning with your current employer or the salary range you expect from this offer.

Answer any of the questions inappropriately and you may hurt your chances for total success. We'll look at each of these situations separately. For each, we'll give possible answers that may be of use to you. Of course, remember that you'll have to tailor your responses to the particular situation.

Salary Request Early On in the Interview

In all cases, you'll do yourself more harm than good by specifically answering this question at this time. Every interviewer knows that some bargaining is to be expected with regard to salary. Asking for salary information early on either shows little regard for the job or little regard for you. Don't give away one of your primary bargaining tools. And remember, you may not have an opportunity to raise your salary for a year or more after accepting their terms. With a request early in the interview, you might answer:

"I'd like to come back to salary negotiations after I understand more fully the job you have to offer."

"I don't think I could be fair to you by answering that right now. May we talk about the ways I will contribute to this company?"

What happens if you do give a specific figure? Well, the dollar figure may be:

1. Too high. You'll be disqualified because they cannot match your price.

2. Too low. Obviously you are not as talented as you say you are. Otherwise, you'd be asking for more money. You're disqualified.

You may be on the money. You may get the job offer after all. If so, don't expect a higher offer than the figure you've given. In fact, if you ask for a higher figure you might be told the interview continued only because the stated figure was the highest figure that could be met. If you press negotiations further, you may be accused of wasting their time by being 'mischievous' or 'devious' in your tactics. And you may find yourself disqualified.

Salary Request in the Middle of the Interview

Again, do not give a definitive answer. If the salary request is made at this time, the interviewer may be taking a more active interest in you. Promote that interest. You could answer with previous examples given, or:

"I'm sure you'll make a fair offer. Were you planning to make an offer?"

They may say that they are not as yet prepared to make you an offer. In effect, they've removed any reason for repeating the request for information. If they do say they're not ready to make an offer, you might respond:

"Well, perhaps we could talk more about the contributions I would make to the company."

Should they say that an offer is possible, you might immediately respond:

"What is the salary range for the position."

You've not pinned them down to a specific figure. Rather, you've established a range where you can fit your dollar figure into. For example, if the range for the position is $32K to $46K, you may realistically respond:

"I would certainly be able to work something out with you in that range. May we continue our discussion of the details of this position?"

Salary Request at the End of the Interview

Expect some request for salary information during some part of your interview. Your best responses will be those which do not lock you into a specific dollar figure. At the end of the interview, you might answer the question with:

"I'm very interested in the position. What is the salary range of the position?"

"I'd like to be able to fit into your salary structure. What is the salary range?"

"I'm sure you'll make a fair offer. What would be a fair offer for this position?"

You must hear a dollar figure or salary range from them before you mention anything. You'll greatly enhance your bargaining power later on with this method. You'll be able to show how you meet and exceed their skill requirements. But you will not be able to get the best salary until you know what they've defined as a range.

Salary History

The only reason the interviewer needs to know your salary history is to bargain with you later on. Don't give them your salary history. Period. Instead, you might answer with:

"My salary history has advanced as I've advanced in my career. Do you see this position as one offering professional advancement?"

"This job is so different from my other jobs that it wouldn't be fair to relate them. Are you planning on making me an offer?"

"Salary history is really so much more than the paycheck. It would be difficult to come up with total compensation right now. What compensation does this position offer?"

The Outright Demand for Current Salary

This is really an unfair question. Still, prospective employers ask the question all the time. Remember, the employer wants you as cheaply as possible. Your aim is to show them those qualities that will help raise their offer.

Your own fundamental concern is watching out for your own best interests. Be polite, be enthusiastic, be honest and don't give in. You might respond:

"My total compensation would need some figuring out. I could schedule another meeting with you to discuss this. Tell me, are you prepared to make me an offer?"

"Compensation deals with so much more than salary. Would you discuss the types of compensation your company offers?"

"I'd have to check the figures, but my total compensation is in the range of $_____ to $_____ ."

If you cite a specific salary range, do not define a dollar spread of $500 or $1000. Give the interviewer a spread of $3000 to $5000. For example, say your total compensation is $26,000 to $31,000. While it is illegal for your current employer to give out your current earnings, you should give a compensation figure near the range(i.e. give $26K–$31K if you earn $24,000).

Compensation is a critical point for you to understand. If you accept a job at a higher salary but have to pay for more of your own benefits, you may find your take–home paycheck lower than expected. Not citing specific dollar figures is not the same as trying to hide information. Do not let the interviewer intimidate you.

If pressed to give, down to the last penny, a specific dollar figure should be given. If you've had to respond this way, and the interviewer says the figure is too high, you might add:

"I do not want to hurt my chances of getting the job. However, I'm looking at all the components of compensation. Since you feel my figure is too high, would you tell me the elements of compensation for this position? I'm sure we could work something out."

You have the responsibility of weighing the job offer. Going into the interview, you must have a tentative breakdown of total compensation. Don't refuse an offer or pursue it less diligently than you should, only to discover you figured the benefits incorrectly. Benefits may include:

1. A company car
2. The pension terms
3. Bonus possibilities
4. Flexible work hours
5. Great advancement opportunities
6. A commute miles closer to home
7. Child care arrangements
8. Fill in the benefits you desire: _____
   _____
   _____

However you plan to approach salary negotiations, you must abide by one cardinal rule.

The Cardinal Rule

Never, never, never accept an offer on the spot. No matter how great the offer sounds, you've got to have at least one day to review the offer. Also, you should fill out the 'Compensation' worksheets in the chapter entitled 'Weighing the Offer' before you respond.

Initial joy may be replaced with minor or major reservations and concerns. Once you've accepted an offer, your bargaining is over.

The Job Interview—Their Questions

The interviewer will have a vitally important question on his or her mind throughout your discussions. You will not be asked this question directly because the question only affects the interviewer.

"Do I like this person?"

Only the interviewer will give the answer. Of course, you are completely responsible for their choice, yes or no. You'll influence their decision. Yet, fairly or unfairly the decision is theirs.

Presenting yourself properly will help determine whether or not you are hired. You certainly need to display the skills they need for the position. But do not negate or lessen the importance of style. Or presentation. Or etiquette.

Sell with style and substance. Follow these simple rules:

1. Allow the interviewer to invite you to sit down. Look for their indication for where you should sit.

2. Ask for their business card, if appropriate. If you ask for a card, be prepared to exchange it with your own. A business card is appropriate for many professions or positions. Even if you are unemployed, having cards printed with your name, address and phone number is acceptable and inexpensive. If possible, include a functional title on the card.

3. Do not lean on their desk.

4. Do not put any of your materials on their desk. There is no reason for your folders or briefcase to be on their desk. If your presentation includes examples, hand the package to the interviewer. Do not assume anything. Ask. "Where may I set out these examples for you?"

5. Respond to a compliment with a thank you. An enthusiastic and sincere thank you.

6. Show a positive attitude about everything. If you were recently fired, show the value of the experience. Never show the pain. If you spill coffee all over your front, show humor about the situation. If you can't handle spilt coffee, can you handle a company crisis?(Why are you drinking coffee during the interview, anyway?)

7. Do not express your achievements with timidity or modesty. These traits may be associated with a weak personality. Their is a difference between arrogance and pride in one's achievements. Never say "Oh, it's nothing.". Instead, you might say "Thank you. I'm very proud of how it helped the team".

8. Never speak of personal problems.

9. Never, not in any fashion, complain about a past employer. If your last employer went bankrupt, locked you out of the office before you could get your personal belongings and didn't pay you for 3 weeks of work, speak of your 'challenges and personal commitment' to the job.

10. Approach everything in the interview as an exercise in what you can do for them, not what they can do for you.

If you follow these rules, you'll suggest to the interviewer that whatever you have to deal with at work will be handled to the benefit of the company.

Listen to the interviewer. Their questions will give you a sense of what problems their company is facing. You may be able to realize what type of person they are looking for. If you can perceive what real problems the questions touch upon, your focused response will be very impressive.

As they talk with you, their main interest will be determining how best you are going to help them. Answer their questions highlighting those perceived needs. Your research should have uncovered pertinent facts about the company that you may use to your benefit. Highlight the solutions and contributions you would offer.

The interviewer may suggest that you lack certain qualities needed for the position. You'll want to react in one of two ways.

First, the interviewer may be incorrect in her assumptions. If so, clarify any perceived misconceptions she has. Speak to whatever issue is at hand. Make sure she understands that you do indeed have the quality she is looking for.

Second, the interviewer may be right. In that case, acknowledge what may not be a strong point. But do not dwell on the fact. Tell the truth and move on. Show how what is lacking is made up for by other strong, valuable qualities, traits and accomplishments. Two strengths may make up for one weakness.

If questions are asked but you do not know how to answer them in the context of the interview, ask for clarification. Ask in a sincere way. No interviewer would perceive this request an insult. Simply tell them that you would like to answer the question as best you can. But, you'd like them to explain further exactly what it is they'd like to know.

Other books list many questions you may encounter during the interview process. They'll tell you to think long and hard about how you'd answer the questions. That advice is not enough.

This book delivers a unique, five–part system for you.

First, the question is listed. Second, you'll gain insight into what information the interviewer wants to gain by asking the question. Third, a sample response is given that you may use as a basis for coming up with your own answers. Fourth, you'll answer the question yourself, expressing your own qualities, traits and accomplishments. And finally, the questions may be cut up like flash cards, allowing you to build confidence by role–playing with a friend or associate.

The interview ultimately determines whether or not you get the job. Special emphasis has been placed on the flash card method of rehearsal. There are questions on each side of these pages. You may want to use a copying machine to make a couple or more sets. (One for the home, one for the train and one for the patient friend?) Copies are beneficial to answer a single question in multiple ways, with different answers for different companies.

Give full effort to this exercise. How you answer those interview questions will deliver the ultimate success or unfortunate failure. Follow these guidelines:

- Relax in a comfortable setting.

- Read through all the questions before writing any of your own answers.

- Begin writing your answers to each question. Answer every question even if the answer has to be 'Does not apply'. Refer to your research throughout the process. Include information about the company, the services, products and problems you've researched.

- When all the answers are written, however long(hours, days) it might take to finish, put the questions aside for a day.

- The next day, review your answers and make any changes you feel are necessary.

- Cut the copies of the originals into flash cards.

You'll then have the answers to most of the questions an interviewer might ask. Can you express verbally what you've written on paper? Once you have your stack of cards, do the following:

- Recruit a friend, family member or associate. Pick a valuable ally who'll play the part of tough interviewer.

- Give them the cards. They should shuffle the cards as many times as they choose.

- They should begin asking the questions.

- Answer the questions. If both of you are satisfied with the content and style of the answer, place a check mark in the box. Repeat the process until all questions are checked off.

- Take your friend out to dinner!

Those Touchy Questions

Specific questions concerning race, age, marital status, handicaps, religion or national origin are not proper questions. We say these questions are not proper, but I hesitate to call them illegal. Since we cannot be sure precisely how these types of questions might be asked, you'll have to decide for yourself how best to respond if the situation arises. Some questions may cross the line of decency while others sit right on that line awaiting a response.

However improper questions may be, you shouldn't refuse to answer any of them unless you plan not to get the job. Remember, you shine through the whole process, get an offer and only then decide what to do, accept or refuse the offer.

You have every right to say no as well as yes. And you may decide to tell the interviewer and the company exactly why your answer is no. They will listen to you. (You may decide to make them listen more than they'd like.)

In all situations leading to the offer, follow their rules. Be pleasant. Cooperate with them and never seem ill–mannered.

Well, it's time now to get into that comfortable setting. Once there, turn to the first interview question and begin.

Question #01:   Why did you apply for this job?
Insight: The interviewer is looking for any sign that you've researched the company. You can, depending on research, cite specifics about the job and how you will meet all challenges.
Example: "This job requires expertise in treating emotionally disabled people. I have considerable expertise in this field. I can meet or surpass all qualifications for the position. Your company is regarded highly and I want to be part of it.
Your Answer:

Question #02:   Who are you?
Insight: You may respond with a question of your own. Or, you might give a broad picture of your strengths, ending with a question back to the interviewer.
Example: "Is there anything in particular that you would like to know?" Or, "I'm a team leader. I like to take charge and motivate a group to achieve greater company goals. What specifics are you particularly interested in?"
Your Answer:

Question #03:   What do you know about this company?
Insight: Your research will pay off handsomely on this one. If you don't know anything about the company, you've needlessly hurt yourself.
Example: "You were founded eleven years ago. You've grown steadily, doubling sales every three years. You've added employees, maintaining the highest sales to employee ratios in the industry. I want to be part of a company that meets and exceeds this type of growth. Do you see this growth continuing in the future?"
Your Answer:

Question #04:   What do you think you'll do in this position?
Insight: Here's where your research is important. If you've written your summary of job qualifications, you can handle this question very specifically. If you have general information, answer in general terms.
Example: "I will assist the Vice President schedule and conduct training for staff. I'll be expected to work in a team environment, while still taking initiative where required. My job requires interaction with all levels of the company. I've got skills to match every requirement and will use them in this position."
Your Answer:

Question #05:   Why did you choose this career?
Insight: The interviewer does not want to hear that you just fell into what you're doing. You should show that your career choice was your own. Show how you've added strengths to your skills throughout your career.
Example: "I've always enjoyed working in a bakery. My grandmother owned a respected bakery when I was young. I've been able to spend my work career learning all aspects of the business. I've helped build community relationships by offering the best products in the market. Would you like examples?"
Your Answer:

Question #06:   Why are you better than the others?
Insight: A tricky question. You do not want to sound arrogant or pompous. Still, you have achievements that you should be proud of and willing to share with the interviewer.
Example: "I'm not aware of the others who have applied for the position. I can say that I am disciplined so that the job gets done well and on time. I will contribute however necessary to meet and exceed expectations."
Your Answer:

Question #07:   What should I know about you?
Insight: This is an innocent question that may hurt or help you. Ask how you may answer specifically. Or, highlight previous career contributions. Do not talk about your personal life.
Example: "What would you like to know?" Or, "I am honest, thorough and able to make every effort necessary to get the job done. What do you consider the biggest priorities of this position?"
Your Answer:

Question #08:   What are your strengths?
Insight: You should not list your past work history. The interviewer wants to know what inherent qualities you possess that will make you able to handle any future assignments.
Example: "I am able to manage my time, prioritizing my work according to management direction. I take pride in my work and always look to gain skills that will make me better."
Your Answer:

Question #09:   What are your weaknesses?
Insight: A favorite question. Say the wrong thing and the interviewer will see why you shouldn't get the job. Say you have no weaknesses and the interviewer won't believe you. You have to show a minor weakness and compensate for it with a strength.
Example: "I guess my greatest weakness is being ill-tempered with people that try to waste my time while I'm trying to get a job done. I don't like gossip and it bothers me when gossip interferes with my schedule. I should be more polite in those situations."
Your Answer:

Question #10: **What are your flaws?**
Insight: The interviewer will gladly allow you to embarrass yourself. You shouldn't bare your soul on this one.
Example: "Like everyone, I've made mistakes. But, I do not repeat those mistakes. I prevent fundamental flaws from being created."
Your Answer:

Question #11: **What do you do best at work?**
Insight: You should consider the things you like to do and do best, then choose the one that most likely fits into this position. You certainly should speak of this accomplishment with pride.
Example: "I'm very proud of my involvement with project teams. I analyze how I will contribute. Based on the goals of management, I gain support as appropriate and make sure that my efforts contribute to the success of the whole project."
Your Answer:

Question #12: **What do you hate to do at work?**
Insight: Remember, though you've researched the position, the interviewer may know more than you do about what you'll be doing. Saying you hate a major responsibility of the job will not help your chances. Answer in general terms. Show how you compensate for that which you do not like doing.
Example: "Some tasks, such as filing documents, seem like a chore. I know keeping good records for the legal department is important. What I make a point of doing is filing during the last twenty minutes of every workday. That way, I can start working with clients first thing each morning and make the legal department happy at the same time."
Your Answer:

Question #13: **What would you say was your biggest accomplishment?**

Insight: Everyone has done something that makes them proud. Your job is to show how accomplishing a similar thing would benefit their company in the future.

Example: "I created a new training manual for our sales managers. Six months after everyone went through the new training our sales were up by 10%. The sales managers directly attributed their success to the manual. I'm very proud of that."

Your Answer:

Question #14: **What would you say was your biggest failure at work?**

Insight: Do not give an example of what you did that brought down your last company! If possible, show a failure that turned into a contribution later on. Speak in general terms.

Example: "I was in charge of changing the hours of staff in the sales office. I listened to one long–term employee and changed hours based on his recommendation. Sales started to slide. I brought the whole team together to invite further discussions. We came up with good solutions. We reopened with all previous hours intact, gave some people flexible hours and initiated part–time schedules. Sales shot up even higher than our original figures."

Your Answer:

Question #15:   What goals do you have?
Insight: You do not want to say that you want the bosses job, or that you want a promotion in 2.4 months, etc.. You want to show that your goals reflect pride in your work. Show that your goals contribute to the company.
Example: "I like to solve problems. I want to learn as much about my profession as possible. I want to continue enjoying the cooperation I've had with my co–workers. Finally, I want to take those skills I have and turn them into profit for the company."
Your Answer:

Question #16:   Where do you want to be in a year?
Insight: Don't tell them anywhere that is away from this lousy job! Show a positive attitude but do not cross the line into arrogance. Show that you want to progress within your environment.
Example: "I've always tried to learn new skills and adapt to new technology. I'd like to make real contributions to my career. I always believe the best comes with the future. Where would you like me to be in a year?"
Your Answer:

Question #17:   How about in 5 years?
Insight: Again, show a progressive attitude. This time, though, you may find it appropriate to add more definition to your previous statement.
Example: "First, I want to complete my last semester and get my college degree. I see that this industry is changing to a more automated environment and I'd like to develop those skills needed to excel as the work place changes. Finally, I'd like to be satisfied that I've taken on more responsibilities with each year and achieved as much as possible."
Your Answer:

Question #18: **Do you think you change jobs too frequently?**
Insight: This question shouldn't be asked unless your résumé show very frequent job moves. If you're asked, stress that you're not out looking for change, but you do want to be challenged in a position.
Example: "I've enjoyed the jobs I've had. I always want to give my best effort to a job. I'm motivated by challenge and believe my best efforts are given to those that demand the best from me. I always want to become better. Does this job offer challenges and growth?"
Your Answer:

Question #19: **What is your salary?**
Insight: Refer back to the chapter 'Preparing for the Interview'. A whole section covers various responses. Just remember, the only reason to ask for your salary is to help them bargain with you.
Example: "Salary is based on so many things. To come up with total compensation would be difficult at this moment. I will certainly get back to you on this point. Tell me, were you planning to make me an offer at this time?"
Your Answer:

Question #20: **What do you want for a salary?**
Insight: Like the previous question, your response will affect you for years to come. Don't give away your primary bargaining chip.
Example: "I'd like to fit into your salary structure. What is that structure?"
Your Answer:

Question #21: **What would you change from your past working history?**

Insight: Ouch! Don't expose any character flaws on this one. Never say that you would have shown more dedication, communicated better or worked more efficiently if you only had the opportunity to do so. The interviewer will assume that if you couldn't do it then you won't do it in the future. Choose an answer that doesn't automatically affect job performance.

Example: "I had an opportunity to move 30 miles closer to my last job. I've always come in early, but being that much closer would have made the commute a lot easier. Where I live now, though, is a very easy commute to your company."

Your Answer:

Question #22: **What kind of student were you?**

Insight: If you were a great student, say so. Tell them your grade average and any awards you received. If you had problems in school, show other qualities that reflect well on you. Give a more generalized response.

Example: "My grades were average to good. I was able to attend school full–time by working a full schedule as well. I feel I received a good education while at the same time developing skills that fit into a career. I've learned to be organized, plan schedules, work at maximum efficiency and get things done by their deadline."

Your Answer:

Question #23:   What was a highlight from school?
Insight: A proud moment should be recounted. Find the relationship between a personal highlight and the job you're after. Of course, don't recount college pranks or crass behavior.
Example: "I was the school newspaper editor. Once, we were ready to go to press when the power on campus went out. We made up teams, quickly gathered all the items we needed to put out the paper and set a course of action. The paper itself and a special insert we had planned were printed in parts in another city. We all got back together and put the paper together. Nobody thought the paper would come out, but it did, and on time."
Your Answer:

Question #24:   Have you ever fired someone?
Insight: If you haven't, answer no. If you say no, you may be asked how you would fire someone. If you have, show how difficult the task was and how you handled the matter with compassion and professionalism.
Example: "Firing someone is always painful to do. In some instances, though, it has to be done. I review company procedures to make sure all regulations are being followed properly. I've sat with individuals throughout the warning process, explaining what would occur at each next step if performance remained unchanged. When the firing takes place, I set up a private meeting with the individual and explain why they'll no longer be part of our organization."
Your Answer:

Question #25:   What does EEO mean?
Insight: EEO is an abbreviation for Equal Employment Opportunity. You will not have to say what year the law was passed or who sponsored the bill. You will say that everyone deserves an equal chance for a job based on qualifications.
Example: "That is an abbreviation for Equal Employment Opportunity. Everyone should be judged based on qualifications for a particular job. We all want to succeed in life and everybody should be given that chance."
Your Answer:

Question #26:   How long will you stay in this job if an offer is made?
Insight: Don't tell them of your planned move to another coast next year or your desire to search for the next, bigger paycheck. Show commitment. Suggest you'd like the same from them.
Example: "I want to stay with a company and a job that offers challenges and increasing responsibilities. I'd like to grow and change as the company grows and changes. This job seems to offer many challenges. How long were you looking for someone to stay in the job?"
Your Answer:

Question #27:   Have you ever been fired?
Insight: If you haven't, say no and be quiet. If you were fired recently, you'll have to say yes. If so, make a brief statement of how you've resolved past mistakes. If possible, put a positive twist on the subject. (Special note: if you were fired in high school or from a job that is no longer on your résumé, you may choose to answer no to the question. Just understand that if the employer finds this out, you'll probably have to explain why you failed to mention it earlier. And you may be fired due to corporate policy.)
Example: "Unfortunately, yes. I had some personal considerations that forced me to come in late at work. I would stay late to make up for this lost time, but the company had very strict hours that had to be followed. Since then, my performance has always been acceptable."
Your Answer:

Question #28:   Why were you laid off?
Insight: A dangerous question. They may be thinking "if you're so great at everything you do, how could the company afford to lose you?". If you were laid off with others you'll be able to minimize any stigma attached.
Example: "The company had to reduce the number of employees to survive in the marketplace. While I contributed in positive ways, the company also looked at years of service and departmental needs. Being a junior member of the staff, there was nothing my bosses could do to change the decisions made by personnel. The company lost some really great people. A total of thirty people were affected."
Your Answer:

Question #29: **What training do you have that qualifies you?**

Insight: Many jobs have definite skills that are used everyday. You may need to use a computer, a copying machine, the fax machine, medical equipment, etc.. You may have to teach or lead a team. Show where you excel. The question may also be looking for information on how well you'll take to being trained in the future. Show them.

Example: "I'm quite good at using and fixing the machines in the office. I understand how important it is to use every resource to work efficiently. I've even taken the initiative to learn to replace fax paper and fix paper jams in the copier. Many times, a repairman doesn't have to come in. I fix the problem."

Your Answer:

Question #30: **How often are you sick?**

Insight: If you are rarely sick, say it proudly. If you take every opportunity to call in sick, give a general answer that doesn't expose a weakness. Rarely will the interviewer ask a reference how often you are sick.

Example: "Certainly nothing more than normal. If a specific number of sick days are allowed each year I do not make plans to use them up."

Your Answer:

Question #31: **What do you think about working overtime?**
Insight: The interviewer wants to know if you'll be a resource during a crunch. Sometimes, especially in salaried positions, the interviewer may want to hire someone who'll work 80 hours per week and receive only one week's paycheck for the effort. Answer that you'll work overtime. Get the job offer. If you are truly concerned about changes to the work schedule, ask for clarification before you sign. If you work out any special overtime compensation, get the facts in writing.
Example: "I have no problem working overtime when needs warrant it. I realize we are in the business of making money. Sometimes we need to put in that extra effort to get the job done. Are there specific overtime considerations I should be aware of?"
Your Answer:

Question #32: **Are you dependable?**
Insight: There is only one answer to this question. You may be asked to follow with an example.
Example: "Absolutely. I define the responsibilities I have to the job or to a project. Then, I work to fulfill any and all responsibilities. I can be depended on in every case."
Your Answer:

Question #33: **Do you have a criminal record?**
Insight: A real tough question if your answer is yes. Give a general answer if at all possible. You may have to explain yourself to the extant of the interviewers' demands.
Example: "Yes, I'm sorry to say, I do. I've overcome those past problems and they'll have no affect on my current job performance."
Your Answer:

Question #34:   Are you always on time?
Insight: In almost every case you should say "Yes, always". If you have chronic problems with tardiness, make every effort to lessen your errors of the past. If you'll not be late in the future and your references won't expose the flaw, answer yes anyway. (Make sure you're on time with your new job!)
Example: "I've had some recent problems with being on time. I made a point of sitting with my supervisor to explain this problem. It was not my intention to be late. Fortunately, we came up with a solution and the matter was resolved."
Your Answer:

Question #35:   Are you bondable?
Insight: Another way of asking if you have a less than honest past. You may be asked to handle large amounts of cash or securities. If you've had no trouble with the law and are a citizen of this country, answer that you are bondable. With a less than illustrious past, you may ask for details on the question. If so, the interviewer may ask for more than you'll want to tell.
Example: "I don't know. I've never applied for such a thing. How does someone become bondable? Would you like me to find out if I am?" Or, "Yes, I imagine so."
Your Answer:

**Question #36:   What things about this job
                    concern you?**
Insight: You have no concerns. You may negotiate items later, but you have no concerns before the offer is made.
Example: "I really cannot think of any concerns I would have. The job and your company offer great opportunities. I'd like to become part of this organization."
Your Answer:

Question #37: Are there personal things that would interfere with your work?

Insight: Interfering with your work and interfering with your schedule may be two very different things. You may have to create a tailored schedule. You'll never have your personal life affect your work. Do you understand the difference?

Example: "No. Working to my best abilities and benefiting the company have always been top priorities."

Your Answer:

Question #38: What things do you do outside of the work place?

Insight: You may speak of a hobby or an organization to which you belong. Show positive personal characteristics that would relate to professional work ethics. Some hobbies, though, may not help your case. For example, do not apply for a position with the humane society and speak of your gun club membership and how much you enjoy killing animals. Answer as appropriate to the situation.

Example: "I coach my sons' little league team and belong to the PTA. I find setting up schedules like I do at work helps make these personal activities possible."

Your Answer:

Question #39: What would be your ideal job?

Insight: Don't describe something that has absolutely no similarities with the job you're applying for. Express qualities that define you as an individual.

Example: "My ideal job would offer challenges each day. I'd enjoy a great working relationship with the rest of the staff. My job would contribute to the company and help raise profits. How does this position fit in with my ideals?"

Your Answer:

Question #40:   **How well do you work with other people?**

Insight: Whether you like working alone or with groups, you want to show you'll cause no problems if you're hired.

Example: "I work very well with people. My previous jobs have often included working long stretches of time by myself. But in every case, when I've interacted with others I've enjoyed it."

Your Answer:

Question #41:   **How well do you work under pressure?**

Insight: This is an important question. Answer this correctly and you'll be able to show you are calm, stable, and level–headed. Give a powerful example of your ability to handle pressure.

Example: "Often times, a short deadline for a project can add pressure. I determine what I have to do, whether day by day or hour by hour. Then, I make sure I complete the small tasks that make up these mini–deadlines. This method relieves most anxieties and pressures associated with meeting deadlines."

Your Answer:

Question #42:   **How would you treat clients?**

Insight: Clients put every dollar in your paycheck. How do you think you treat them?

Example: "The client is the single most important part of company success. A company survives and prospers according to how well we treat clients. They deserve every consideration."

Your Answer:

206

Question #43: **What leadership qualities do you have?**

Insight: You may be asked to give examples. Most often, though, the interviewer wants to hear more about your personal characteristics, the fundamental qualities you possess to lead.

Example: "Leadership qualities are certainly learned experiences. To lead, you have to motivate in others those things that motivate you. Listening to the opinions of others, following good advice and motivating a team toward a common goal are all qualities of leadership. Of course, leadership qualities continues to accrue with a lifetime of learning."

Your Answer:

Question #44: **What type of supervisor are you?**

Insight: If you are applying for a supervisory position, you'd better say you're damn good. If you're not trying to become a supervisor, speak of your competence and success at working with others.

Example: "I've been more of a team player than a supervisor. On the team, though, I find that people look to me for help. I think that's because I listen to their problems and suggest solid solutions."

Your Answer:

Question #45: **Have you ever worked for yourself?**
Insight: The interviewer may have two opposite reasons for asking this question. First, they may like someone who is able to take care of himself. Second, they may fear you'll strike out again and leave the company. You'll have to analyze the situation and answer accordingly.
Example: "Yes, I have. I find having worked for myself and for a large company gives me multiple perspectives on how an organization works. Working for myself, I realize that every action affects something else. With a large company, I know my job affects the rest of the company."
Your Answer:

Question #46: **What are 5 talents you have?**
Insight: Here is where humor is not called for. If you respond "Only 5?" the interview might say "O.K., give me 10". You know your qualifications. Your research suggests those things important to the job. Combine the two.
Example: "I'm a team player. I can analyze a problem and offer multiple solutions. I treat clients well and am loyal to them. I'm able to diffuse conflicts in the office and I always look for ways to make a product more profitable.
Your Answer:

Question #47: **Why are you looking for a job?**
Insight: If you have a job, you want to better yourself. If you're out of a job, you want to work. Assess the interviewers' company to determine what is most needed and sell those points.
Example: "I've worked for a number of years at a large company. My department numbers 250 people. I'm looking to contribute to a company where the affects of my work are immediately known. The size of your company demands that everyone assume responsibility for their actions. I like that."
Your Answer:

Question #48: **What things did your last employer do wrong?**
Insight: A long-standing rule is to never criticize a former employer. The rule still stands. Say you can't think of anything or come up with something that won't jeopardize your chances.
Example: "I've really respected my company. Recently, they decided to continue allowing smoking on the floor. I'm not thrilled with that since I don't smoke."(And neither does the interviewer!)
Your Answer:

Question #49:   There are missing periods in your work history. What were you doing?

Insight: This question shouldn't be asked since you've accounted for all the years back to college. Correct? Don't forget that years spent at home can be given a title. If time is missing, explain it as a period of research. You should speak the truth, but speak it to your advantage.

Example: "I've been in the same industry for twelve years. I always want to learn more and do more so I took that time to research two other industries. After a year of researching the other industries and visiting companies around the region, I decided I could still make my best contributions to our industry."

Your Answer:

Question #50:   Are you willing to move?

Insight: Though you've lived in the same house your whole life and plan to be buried in the back yard, don't say you'd refuse to listen to the offer.

Example: "I'd be willing to consider it. Many things are affected by a move and I'd have to look at each of them. I'd weigh these things against the contributions I would make with the job. Do you anticipate relocation?"

Your Answer:

Question #51:   How did you work while you were in school?

Insight: If they ask you this question, they should be impressed that you handled both work and school at the same time. Be proud of the personal traits you have that enabled you to succeed.

Example: "I knew it was going to be tough. First, I talked to a couple of employers in the area. I agreed to accept a job that allowed me to work on two different schedules. Then, I selected classes that fit into these schedules. Studying and taking tests was hard, but I developed weekly goals that moved papers and projects to resolution."

Your Answer:

Question #52:   **How do you handle pressure?**
Insight: An earlier question asked how well you would work under pressure. With that question you may give a specific example. This question, though, allows you to stress the many personality traits you have.
Example: "First, I stay calm. I accept the situation as a challenge. I analyze the situation, asking for advice where necessary. I deal with each of the problems there are. Finally, I handle the situation in whatever way I may benefit the company."
Your Answer:

Question #53:   **Give me an example of a crisis. How did you handle it?**
Insight: They really don't care what the crisis was. They want to know what steps you'll take if and when you face difficult and crisis situations.
Example: "We were converting a new system. A crisis developed on Friday night which necessitated a core group staying through the weekend. I came up with a workable plan. We split the group in half, one group working Saturday and the other on Sunday. We created a buddy system, where the Sunday people would take care of the Saturday peoples' appointments and vice versa. We got everyone together on Sunday night, families included, and celebrated our success with a barbecue. Plus, Monday morning I was able to tell senior management that this team prevented a loss of $75,000 from occurring."
Your Answer:

Question #54:   Do you like working alone?
Insight: Your response will depend on what the job offers, whether a team or solitary environment. Whichever way you answer, don't answer in such a way that excludes one of your choices.
Example: "I can concentrate for long periods of time and have no problems working alone. Of course, if I'm needed for meetings or for support on a project I'll participate gladly."
Your Answer:

Question #55:   We have a policy of giving drug tests.
   Will you take one?
Insight: If you want the job you're probably going to have to say yes. Whether you have a drug problem or not, consider the example before deciding to simply answer yes to this question.
Example: "Yes, I will. I would like to know how you protect the confidentiality of the results. Also, I understand that different foods or cold remedies or other medications may affect results. If the result is in error, will there be additional testing to disprove the error?"
Your Answer:

Question #56:   Will you travel for us?
Insight: Similar to the moving question. Here, though, you'll want to stress your flexibility. If you are concerned about travel, do two things. First, get the job offer. Second, ask to come to an agreement regarding the specific travel requirements. And remember, three nights away from home is work for you. Compensation should find its way into your discussions. (You do not want to pay out–of–pocket cash only to find you'll be reimbursed four months later.) If you are new to travelling on the job, know that the glamour wears thin quickly.
Example: "Yes, I would. What kind of a travel schedule would this job require?" Later, during the salary negotiations, "How does the company handle travel compensation?"
Your Answer:

Question #57:   Where do you get your motivation
**   to do your job?**
Insight: A short, simple answer is all that is required. Read the example. Say it if you like.
Example: "I like to succeed in everything I do. There is no greater motivation for me than that."
Your Answer:

Question #58: **What kind of things do you do on your own time?**

Insight: A similar question to one stated earlier. This question may come as a result of genuine interest in you. Many employers find that activities outside the office define how well you'll perform on the job. Consider your answer carefully.

Example: "I'm active in many things. I take a couple of classes each year to learn something new. My husband and I try to maintain an active social life with family and friends. We also take part in as many school activities as possible. Just like at work, scheduling activities helps get them all accomplished."

Your Answer:

Question #59: **What are your hobbies?**

Insight: Similar to the previous question. Here you are asked to give an example. Do not mention a hobby that might offend the interviewer. You may not want to explain that you're an activist promoting solar windmills to the oil company executive.

Example: "I collect old toys. It's great to understand how people lived in the past. You can tell a lot about who we are by understanding where we've been. I also like the research to determine value. Age, manufacturer, condition and paint affect value. You've got to know your stuff or you'll lose money."

Your Answer:

Question #60:   **How do you solve a problem?**
Insight: The interviewer wants to understand how you move a situation to resolution. Show the way in brief, well-defined steps.
Example: "First, I identify the whole problem. Next, I determine if the problem can be broken up into pieces that can be addressed separately. I'll then discuss the best approach for a solution with my manager. I'll ask for guidance and help as necessary. I'll do any research needed to cover all sides of the issue. Finally, I'll combine all of the above to arrive at the solution to the problem."
Your Answer:

Question #61:   **How did you finance your education?**
Insight: The interviewer doesn't want to hear that your parents wrote you a check, with an extra $5,000 for clothes. You do not have to share all sordid details of how it happened. Simply show that you are resourceful.
Example: "Well, I wrote up a list of the costs I knew about. I figured out how much money I had to cover those costs and how much remained to be found. I spent time with my student counselor and with my parents to figure out the rest. I did receive some scholarships and a student grant. My parents also helped."
Your Answer:

Question #62:   **Tell me, what makes you tick?**
Insight: Your answer might lead in any direction with this one. Your best bet is to ask "Is there something specific you'd like to know?". If they answer no, show positive personal traits. Be brief.
Example: "I'm someone who wants to build a better future. I work at getting better all the time. I relax and enjoy the process of getting there. If I make a contribution I'm satisfied."
Your Answer:

Question #63: **How do you define success?**
Insight: Look back at your strengths you identified in the chapter 'Defining Your Strengths'. One strength may be turned into a general definition of success.
Example: "I define success as overcoming obstacles or meeting self-defined goals to achieve what you want in life. At the same time, success comes with honesty and integrity."
Your Answer:

Question #64: **Are you motivated?**
Insight: Show you get things done while still playing by the rules.
Example: "Yes, I am. Things should get done in the best way possible. Naturally, I'm aware of company policies and motivate myself with those policies in mind."
Your Answer:

Question #65: **Can you tell me about this company?**
Insight: A great question, especially since you know so much about the company. With your research, this question is a piece of cake. Give specifics as befits your cause.
Example: "Certainly, I'm impressed with the growth you've experienced over the last three years. I also admire some of the new products you've introduced recently. May I talk about one of these subjects?"
Your Answer:

Question #66:   **What machines can you use?**
Insight: The interviewer wants to know how much you'll depend on other members of her staff. Tell what you can do. If you can learn a skill before you begin the job you may want to include that also. (Remember the story about the actor who got the job because he could ride a horse though he'd never saddled up?) If you say you can do it, make sure you can live up to your words by the first day of employment.
Example: "I'm familiar with most office equipment. I've used various copiers, the fax machine, multi–party telephones, typewriters and personal computers. Are there other machines you use?"
Your Answer:

Question #67:   **How important is a title to you?**
Insight: You'll answer best if you know beforehand how important titles are to the company. Play the middle road if you don't know.
Example: "Titles can be very important defining an organization. Or they may serve only as a general indication of job functions. I'm comfortable with either approach."
Your Answer:

Question #68:   **If you could do anything you wanted, what job would suit you?**
Insight: Don't dismiss the job being offered as the last thing you'd do if you had your choice. Talk about personal traits you'd use in the job.
Example: "I'd like to be project leader for a critical task. In truth, I think I'll be qualified to do that in a few years. I'm always trying to add skills and develop qualities that enhance my ability to lead."
Your Answer:

Question #69:   What do your parents do?
Insight: If you think it will help your case, tell the interviewer and use specifics. If your parents professional lives conflict with your perception of what the interviewer would like to hear, give a general answer. Of course, remember that you may name a company and leave off a job title.
Example: "Both my parents are professionals working full time. My mom works at a bank. Dad works for a computer firm."
Your Answer:

Question #70:   How would you react if your boss treated you unfairly?
Insight: They want to know if you'll follow procedures, go through proper channels and cause minimal disruption. Show that you are a professional.
Example: "First, I'd take my concerns to my boss. I'd explain why I felt the way I did and ask if I was incorrect in my thinking. If I felt a really major problem existed, I'd go through company–defined channels to resolve it. I've never really had a problem like this. Some days are just pressure–filled. I don't take a rough day personally."
Your Answer:

Question #71:   Do you have references?
Insight: Of course you do. You'll even be able to give them names, addresses and telephone numbers. Follow the procedures outlined in the chapter entitled 'References'.
Example: "Yes, I do. I have a list of names, addresses and telephone numbers. I can give you this list now or later, whichever you prefer."
Your Answer:

Question #72:   **How do you define quality?**
Insight: There are many ways to answer this question. Show the interviewer how you'll get clients, keep clients and provide exceptional service that is respected and admired.
Example: "Clients find quality in the products they buy and the people they buy them from. Quality is giving the client what they need now and continually providing a high level of service so they'll come back over and over again."
Your Answer:

Question #73:   **You change jobs often. You're not
                       very stable, are you?**
Insight: Prove them wrong. You are stable. Other considerations necessitated change. It is that simple.
Example: "On the contrary, I'm very stable. I think instability is the result of not having any focus in life. As you see, each change I've made has been progressive. Each new job has brought greater challenges. Do you feel I'll be challenged in this position?"
Your Answer:

Question #74:   **If you received a bonus, what would
                       your do with the money?**
Insight: Self-control is what they are interested in. Don't show a wanton disregard for the value of money.
Example: "Well, it would depend on the size of the bonus. If it was small, I'd take my family out to dinner and buy each of us a small gift. With a large bonus, I'd look at things like getting ahead on the mortgage, paying small debts, etc.. I'd still buy each of us a small gift as well."
Your Answer:

Question #75:   **Are you happy with the major you chose in college?**

Insight: Your only answer is yes. You don't want to suggest you'll always be wandering through life searching for better jobs 'if only' your degree was different.

Example: "Yes, I am. The courses were broad–based enough to give me many perspectives on the business world. Still, my major gave me the discipline to set goals and achieve results."

Your Answer:

Question #76:   **Do you have your degree?**

Insight: If you do have a degree, answer yes. Do not give long, specific explanations that may result in a biased attitude from the interviewer. Another words, don't let your specificity narrow your job opportunities. If your answer is no, say so without saying the word 'no'

Example: "I've had to earn a living since high school. I've attended classes and received technical training as I've moved up in the business world. As yet, though, I'm still making my way towards a degree."

Your Answer:

Question #77:   **How do you define an incompetent worker?**

Insight: If you know company policies, define incompetence as traits that go against those policies. Don't tell a story about specific workers, colleagues or former bosses.

Example: "A good worker takes advantage of the resources around her. The supervisor, the company library, fellow associates and one's own background all support your ability to do a good job. An incompetent worker doesn't use the resources given to her."

Your Answer:

Question #78:   **Tell me about some of your experiences?**
Insight: Tell any experience that will reflect well on the qualities you'll bring to the job. Perhaps you might ask what things you'd be doing in the first few months on the job so that you might focus your answer.
Example: "I've had many experiences that show how I'd contribute to a company. Would you tell me what the immediate concerns are for this job? I would gladly relate my experiences to those concerns."
Your Answer:

Question #79:   **How did your last job relate to the goals of the company?**
Insight: Whatever your job, show how you played a part in company goals. If you haven't played a part, why were you working?
Example: "I was part of a team environment that had schedules to meet and jobs to get done on time. I knew what my manager and the company wanted from me. When we all pulled together, each effort supported the success of the group."
Your Answer:

Question #80:   **Are you organized? How so?**
Insight: The company wants to know if you'll be wasting their time and money. Show how your organizational skills actually save money.
Example: "I organize a schedule according to day–to–day tasks and special projects that have set deadlines. I make sure I'll have all the resources available to get the job done on time and within budget. Wasting time hurts the company and it hurts me."
Your Answer:

Question #81: **Couldn't I find someone with your skills anywhere?**

Insight: Tell them again how you meet all skills requirements. Then add those extra qualities you have, like attitude and enthusiasm. Show them what special characteristics you have that will lead to the best success.

Example: "I'm not so sure. I can manage a project. I can get the job done. I have each skill you're looking for and something more. I am looking to make valuable contributions to the company. Respecting my peers and being respected by them, giving praise where due and always learning new skills are important to me. Every job grows in different ways. I can face new challenges and meet that growth. Do you think these are the values that all skilled workers have?"

Your Answer:

Question #82: **What is the most recent book you've read. Why did you read it?**

Insight: You won't want to give the name of the latest romance novel or 'beach book' you've read. Always add value to everything you do. Be prepared to be asked questions about the book. If you don't read anything but mindless literature you'd better change your habits.

Example: "I've recently read 'The Bear' by William Faulkner. I like classic American fiction, Faulkner in particular. Like this industry, his work has so many layers of meaning. It helps me see that I should look at all levels of an issue before coming to any decisions about whether things are right or wrong."

Your Answer:

Question #83:   **Is this job better, the same or worse than your last one?**

Insight: Never worse. The job should either be the same with chances for growth or better than what you had last. If you say worse, what are you running away from? More responsibilities?

Example: "I'd call this job different. Some tasks will be the same while others will be more challenging. I'm sure I can handle all aspects of the job. This job will give me the opportunity to learn more about the field while contributing in many ways to benefit the company."

Your Answer:

Question #84:   **Do you do what you're told?**

Insight: Do not say that you should be 'asked', not 'told'. The interviewer only wants to be assured that you won't be a problem to the rest of the staff.

Example: "I take direction well. I figure the boss has reasons for telling me what to do. Do you have concerns that I wouldn't contribute?"

Your Answer:

Question #85:   **Rate yourself. From a one to a ten, what are you?**

Insight: Show self-confidence, not arrogance. Don't say 10 or you'll be considered a liar. Say anything below a seven and it's over. A 7, 8 or 9 are your only choices.

Example: "I'd give myself a solid 8. Every year I learn more, use new technologies and add to my skills. There is always room to learn more, contribute more and achieve higher goals. What do you think I am?"

Your Answer:

Question #86: **If I told you your interviewing skills stink, what would you tell me?**

Insight: Don't blow your chances with this one. The interviewer probably likes you and wants to see if you'll become flustered. Stay calm and you'll pass this test.

Example: "I'd ask you for specifics. If I felt the problem was due to miscommunication I'd try to clear it up. If what you told me was accurate, I'd ask your advice on how I could learn better interviewing skills. That way, I wouldn't let the problem happen again." Then, with a smile, "Do you think my skills stink?".

Your Answer:

Question #87: **Do you need to be pampered?**

Insight: Say or suggest you do and you're out.

Example: "No. I don't."

Your Answer:

Question #88: **Are you opinionated?**

Insight: Stay in the middle on this one. Saying you are strongly opinionated may work in some interviews. Or you may be considered a problem–maker, not a problem–solver.

Example: "Naturally, I do have opinions. There are usually right and wrong ways to do something. If I was doing a job that didn't seem to be based on sound decisions, I'd review my concerns with my supervisor to get their perspective. Of course, I'd follow their lead."

Your Answer:

224

Question #89:   Sell me this desk?
Insight: No, not the desk! I thought I was going to have to sell you a pen! If you're applying for a job that deals directly with the client, this question may come up. (More and more positions deal directly with the client. Don't disregard this question.) The interviewer wants to see your skills in action as well as determining how well you can keep your composure. Sell the features and the benefits.
Example: "Sir, you need a desk that will offer long–term value. Our desk offers a large writing surface, laminated to give you years of service. The drawer space is designed to accommodate new technologies used in the work place. With value you look for good price. Our price is competitive with other manufacturers while offering added benefits others simply do not offer. Are you looking for the best, most affordable desk on the market?"
Your Answer:

Question #90:   Would you step on your boss to
**   get ahead?**
Insight: You may be speaking to your next boss. Remember, do unto others ...
Example: "No, I wouldn't. If I had that type of attitude, I'd have to expect someone would also do that to me. I wouldn't tolerate that and I wouldn't do it."
Your Answer:

Question #91: **How would you do something that had never been done before?**

Insight: Will you handle things, even the unknown, according to establish procedures? Or will you run off willy-nilly without regard for the company?

Example: "If I was alone and had to make an immediate decision, I'd do what I thought was best for the company. Otherwise, I'd talk with my manager and look for their direction."

Your Answer:

Question #92: **What won't you do for us?**

Insight: Don't establish yourself as standing apart from the team. Still, your personal traits are important and should be used in responding to a question such as this one.

Example: "I won't lie. I won't steal. I think I have values that match the values of your company."

Your Answer:

Question #93: **Your jobs are not really impressive for someone of your age, are they?**

Insight: First, you'll want to qualify their concerns. Then, you may answer. Don't think about the discriminatory tone until after you're offered the job. You can always turn down a job offer. (It feels good to turn down an offer from someone who doesn't deserve your talents.)

Example: "Different companies use titles that mean different things. I have solid experience in each of the areas you are looking for strengths in. I think doing a great job at whatever you do is important. What would you consider impressive?"

Your Answer:

Question #94: **Tell me your most embarrassing moment?**

Insight: Your most embarrassing moment did not happen on the job. Remember that. Also, make sure you don't expose a character flaw. For example, don't tell a story that shows how you deliberately hurt someone with a sexist remark.

Example: "Last summer I got into a car that looked exactly like mine. While I was trying to fit the key into the ignition, the car owner came at me screaming and a crowd formed around the car. I was mortified."

Your Answer:

Question #95: **What do you think of me?**

Insight: Again, this may be your future boss. Give a brief answer and be quiet.

Example: "I think you're tough but fair."

Your Answer:

Question #96: **What would you do if I yelled at you? How would you react?**

Insight: If you are yelled at in a job, you'll have different options available which are different than why this question is being asked. The interviewer wants to know how easily you'll lose control when times are tough. Show you can be tough back at the interviewer.

Example: "Days can be tough. I'd figure you had a really rough day and were letting off some steam. I'd also listen to your underlying message and correct anything I'd done wrong. Of course, if you yelled at me repeatedly, we'd come to some resolution."

Your Answer:

Question #97: **The last guy from your company stole from us? Is this a common trait at your company?**
Insight: Another test. Defend yourself. Even more importantly, defend the company.
Example: "I can assure you that I do not share that trait. I'm not aware of anything like that happening in my department or division. The company reviews employees as thoroughly as possible."
Your Answer:

Question #98: **Do you want to work or get ahead?**
Insight: The interviewer is looking for how you'll contribute to the company. Show that the company comes first. Show that an employee is rewarded through efforts made.
Example: "I think giving everything to your work leads to success. Sure, I'd like to get ahead, but I'm willing to put in the work effort and ethic to get there."
Your Answer:

Question #99: **Whom do you admire?**
Insight: Traits you admire in others are probably the same traits you'll aspire to in your own life. Be sappy if you like, but show a connection of personality traits to the job.
Example: "I admire my dad a lot. He had to raise four kids after my parents were divorced. He gave each of us daily and weekly schedules which helped us accomplish everything we all wanted to do. We were able to survive as a family because he pulled us together, through both good times and bad."
Your Answer:

Question #100: **If you could change just one thing about yourself, what would it be and why?**

Insight: This if simply another way of asking if you are going to cause any problems in the office. Remember, the interviewer probably knows all the staff. If you speak of something that would offend a highly valued employee, you may be in trouble. Try to keep your remarks short and away from work habits.

Example: "During summer break as a sophomore in college, I went overseas. Instead of coming home when I should have, I stayed an extra two weeks. During that two weeks, I broke my leg and ended up on crutches for a couple months. I think I would have been better off coming home."

Your Answer:

Question #101: **You have done so much in so little time, according to your résumé. Why would you want to leave your current job?**

Insight: As long as you haven't lied on your résumé, you'll be fine. When you wrote your résumé, you were probably amazed by how much you've accomplished, both personally and professionally. Just let the interviewer know that the only way we grow as human beings is to learn new things and accept new challenges.

Example: "First of all, thank you for the compliment. I've always tried to do my best at my job and get involved with any changes or new things that occur in the office. I think having one job for a whole career is fine as long as you can learn more and do more every year. There aren't many people in my office. Your business is about twice as large as where I am now and I believe you'd offer twice the opportunities."

Your Answer:

The Job Interview—Your Questions

Your questions are vitally important. You'll demonstrate how well you've researched the job and the company. You'll convey personal attributes such as integrity and dependability. You'll ask those questions that properly fit into the meeting. As the interviewer will certainly not ask you every question from the previous chapter, you should not subject the interviewer to an unwelcome barrage of questions.

Still, you need to know as much as possible about the company and the job to make a proper evaluation. If the interviewer covers material during the interview, don't be disrespectful and ask for continued repetition of a point. Clarification is certainly permissible, as is a graciousness about it.

You do not want to give a sense that you are directing the interview. Act politely. Show good manners. Show how flexible you can be. Never show signs of resignation. Learn how to maintain eye–to–eye contact.

One of the best ways to lose a job offer is with a bluff. Never ask for a job offer with the threat of another fictitious job offer. Somehow the interviewer can sense this fraud and will wish you well, ending the interview. You'll have no recourse. Therefore, use the truth. You'll never have to apologize for it.

Of course, if you have one or more job offers your tactics may be different. You may decide that a particular job offers the most opportunity. You also know that other offers won't wait weeks and months for a response. In this case, asking your best choice to make an offer is important.

First, you should follow all the regular processes outlined in this book. If your first meeting is a success, ask if you may schedule your next session for as soon as possible. You may tell the interviewer that your desire is to work at a company where you may make your most outstanding contribution. You may also tell them that another company, or other companies, has recognized your value and made a job offer. You are flattered with those offers, but you are very interested in how you could benefit this company. Be polite and ask for what you need. For example:

"I fully understand your need to choose the best candidate. I am committed to making a decision on the other offer(s) by (date). Before I do, though, I'd like to explore further what seems to be the tremendous opportunities offered by your company. Is there a way we could work this out?"

Look at what you've conveyed with that response:

1. You've complemented the interviewer.
2. You've said you are in demand.
3. You've said you're responsible (to the other companies).
4. You've complemented their company.
5. You respect the interviewers' time, allowing them any and every opportunity to set up another meeting before your deadline(s).

With all the exercises from this book completed, you'll have a strong reference for what you're looking for in a great job. The following questions reflect many of the areas of interest you'll have when looking for the best job.

Each set of questions is set up in the same flash card manner as in the previous chapter. You may or may not have your own reasons for asking these questions. Choose those questions that specifically apply to you and your interests. Write the questions you want to ask and write them in your own language.

Whereas the interviewer may ask any and all questions, you may choose to ask one, several or many questions. Be bold. Ask what you want. Find out what you need to know.

Question # 01: **How does this job affect the department?**

Reason to Ask: You may have held a previous position where your efforts were what kept the office going each day. Depending on the size or style of the company you're applying to, the crucial and immediate importance of the job may vary. You should decide what role you want to play in the office. Listen for any hidden meanings in their response.

Your Question and Reason to Ask:

Question # 02: **What do you think the learning curve is for this job?**

Reason to Ask: You may prefer a job where pressure comes with direct experience, allowing weeks or months to fully meet expectations. The company may expect high output on the first day of employment.

Your Question and Reason to Ask:

Question # 03: **How does the job fit into the organization chart? May I see a chart?**

Reason to Ask: A Vice President in one company may be a Specialist in another company. Likewise, the layers of workers and management may be small or vast. You may not want to find yourself 5th in line to the top today and 12th in line tommorrow.

Your Question and Reason to Ask:

233

A ① **Question # 04:   Is this position new or vacated?**
Reason to Ask: With a new position you have more opportunities to define the responsibilities of the job. You may be able to rewrite the job description as well as the salary range.
Your Question and Reason to Ask:

A ① **Question # 05:   How long has the position been open?**
Reason to Ask: An important question. If the position hasn't been filled for months you'll want to know why. Try to find out if something is wrong with the department. Is the boss unbearable? Did the company put a freeze on hiring(and raises and promotions)? Is the job unimportant to the organization?
Your Question and Reason to Ask:

Question # 06:   What happened to the last person who held this job?
Reason to Ask: Was the work too overwhelming and pressure–filled for one person to handle? Did the person stay with the company, moving up to a more enviable position? Do you sense that promotions are attained after a short or long period of good performance on the job? Do you get a sense of what will ultimately happen to you if you accept this job?
Your Question Reason to Ask:

Question # 07: **Do you promote from within?**
How does that process work?

Reason to Ask: Similar to the previous question. Here, though, you are specifically asking what will happen to you in the future. Beware of the implications in the question. An eagerness in knowing how quickly you can leave a position may signal that you're not the right person for the job. If you ask this question, present it in such a way that shows you want to grow with the company. Do not give any indication that interest in the present offering won't last for a long period of time.

Your Question and Reason to Ask:

Question # 08: **Is the company going through any major plans or changes I should be aware of?**

Reason to Ask: You may be hired tommorrow and be asked to relocate next month. You may accept an attractive job offer today and be laid–off two months later due to restructuring. You'll do your research. Add to your decision–making process by asking this question.

Your Question and Reason to Ask:

Question # 09: **Do you see ways I could benefit the department outside of day to day activities?**

Reason to Ask: Show that you have other skills that could be incorporated into the position. And remember, if the company wants those extra skills to reap their benefits, you'll have a bargaining chip when negotiating your salary. After all, if you're willing to add significantly to the job, shouldn't you want more compensation for those efforts?

Your Question and Reason to Ask:

Question # 10:   What do you like the most about the company?

Reason to Ask: You may ask this question to determine whether your personality fits in with the company. If the interviewer says she admires the highly structured environment and you love a loose structure, you may want to consider whether the company is a viable choice for you.

Your Question and Reason to Ask:

Question # 11:   How do you evaluate job performance?

Reason to Ask: Do you enjoy fighting for a raise each year, initiating the process every time? If you were not to ask for a raise, would you still be earning the same salary five years later? Is it important to you to have a performance review and raise every January? This question is important to ask. The company has no responsibility to ensure that you're happy with your salary, that the salary keeps up with and exceeds the rate of inflation, etc.. You do.

Your Question and Reason to Ask:

Question # 12:   Are there training programs you offer?

Reason to Ask: Are there skills you need or want which the company will help you get? Will they offer seminars in–house? Will they pay for certain classes at the community college? If you have no plans to participate in training you do not have to ask this question. But if somebody with more skills gets the next promotion, you won't complain. Right?

Your Question and Reason to Ask:

Question # 13:   Do you offer any type of reimbursement for education? How does that work?

Reason to Ask: Do you need to finish certain classes to get a college degree? Would the company fulfill all their job requirements if you got the degree? Would they give you six months or a year, or more, to finish? Might reimbursement come in the form of flexible hours? The employee handbook will answer many of these questions. Ask for an employee handbook or company literature.

Your Question and Reason to Ask:

Question # 14:   What are the growth opportunities in this company?

Reason to Ask: When you ask the question, look for the reaction. The interviewer may tell you the exciting opportunities available. Or, he may indicate(with facial expression) that he thinks you're after a promotion before you've even received the job offer. If you are concerned with their reaction, clarify 'growth opportunities' as education, volunteering for special projects, seminars, computer classes, etc..

Your Question and Reason to Ask:

Question # 15:   How does the company perceive itself in the market place?

Reason to Ask: Do you care if your product is the best in the industry? If you get any type of bonus which is based on sales, do you want clients lining up for purchases? Do you want to have to chase clients and leads? Corporate prestige affects you personally. Winning comes more easily if the company shares your ambitions.

Your Question and Reason to Ask:

Question # 16: Are there any skills I seem to lack which I could comment on? Do you have any reservations that I could respond to?

Reason to Ask: If the interviewer doesn't plan to offer you the job, wouldn't you like to know why? If the interviewer bases objections on misconceptions, correct and clarify their misgivings.

Your Question and Reason to Ask:

Question # 17: How does overtime affect the position?

Reason to Ask: If you'll be paid by the hour, would you like to work ten extra hours each week so that you can buy a computer for your home? If you're a salaried employee, will you work sixty hours weekly with no bonus or promotion potential? Is extensive travel considered overtime?

Your Question and Reason to Ask:

Question # 18: Who are the other people I would be working with? How do we support each other?

Reason to Ask: Hopefully, you'll request meeting your future co-workers. These are the people you'll spend 50% of your waking hours with each week. Do you want to do battle every day to get a special project off the ground? Meet these people and assess their personalities. Make sure you are either compatible or able to control job satisfaction.

Your Question and Reason to Ask:

Question # 19:   May I meet those people?
Reason to Ask: It is doubtful the final interviewer would refuse your request. If you go through an initial screening with personnel, don't expect to meet co-workers at that time. You should look to set up an appointment with the department manager. Then, you may meet those people. If the department manager puts off your request, ask again at the end of the interview. Meet your future co-workers then or later, but meet them before you say yes to the job offer.
Your Question and Reason to Ask:

Question # 20:   May I see the area where I'd be working?
Reason to Ask: Not only people make a work environment enjoyable. Would you enjoy a closed-in, windowless area shared by 12 other employees? How about if everyone except you smoked? Determine what is important to you. The plants, the brand of computers, the layout of desks, fax and copying machines— all influence your happiness on the job.
Your Question and Reason to Ask:

Question # 21:   How do you handle raises and promotions? What is your review process?
Reason to Ask: Different than other previous questions. This question specifically asks about position and money. If you accept a reasonable salary, the company(especially smaller ones) will be more than willing to keep you at that salary for years if you'll let them. Meanwhile, your rent has gone up and inflation has added 6% each year to your grocery bill. Company literature may answer these questions. If not, ask.
Your Question and Reason to Ask:

Question # 22: **What do you consider to be the long–range goals of the company?**

Reason to Ask: Does the interviewer enjoy the work and the products? Is the company planning to phase out the products you love and put you in charge of a dreaded task? Whether using questions, company literature or business and investment publications, make sure the company has long–range plans that match your own.

Your Question and Reason to Ask:

Question # 23: **Are there skills I have which you think might not be utilized in this position?**

Reason to Ask: This is another way of finding out if you're overqualified or underqualified. Except that 'over' and 'under' are not part of your vocabulary. You are simply differently qualified. If the interviewer likes you and wants you, she'll do whatever is possible to find an appropriate position for you. This question may also allow you to rewrite the position more to your interests and desires.

Your Question and Reason to Ask:

Question # 24: **How do you feel this company is rated as compared with others in the industry?**

Reason to Ask: With your research you'll know the ranking number. You want two other pieces of information. First, you'll want to know if the interviewer is up on his own company. Second, you'll want to listen to his perspective on those statistics. You may actually gain leads on other companies that you should research and apply to for employment. Professionally said, you may tell the interviewer more about the company than he knows and show that you're an ideal candidate.

Your Question and Reason to Ask:

Question # 25: Are there ways this position will change? How?

Reason to Ask: Have you ever reached home, only to find the sandwich you picked up was pastrami instead of roast beef? You ordered roast beef. The sandwich should be roast beef! When you order anything, you expect to get what you've ordered. The same thing happens with a job. Yes, you'll grow. But you accept a position based on what you agree to beforehand. Do you want to spend 90% of your day filing, when you thought the filing would take a maximum of 10% of your time?

Your Question and Reason to Ask:

Question # 26: Will the company be introducing any new technologies which will change the position?

Reason to Ask: If the technology group is outfitting the entire department next month, you'll want to know about it. You may not have a certain skill today. If the interviewer knows what new technologies are coming, you may want to volunteer to get preliminary training to qualify for the job. Gaining skills is easy. Knowing which skills to get is the hard part.

Your Question and Reason to Ask:

Question # 27: Do you have a written job description?

Reason to Ask: Some companies will let you run the department at a clerical salary if you'll do it for them. Review a job description before you accept the offer. If no job description exists, offer to write one and have the appropriate representative of the company sign and agree to it. Your raises and promotions will be easier to come by if you can prove exactly how you have exceeded requirements. If you have no written requirements, you have absolutely no proof that you've exceeded anything.

Your Question and Reason to Ask:

Question # 28:   What are your standard hours of work?
Reason to Ask: This may be a great question. The response you receive may influence how you'll pursue a variety of work schedules. In today's market, flexible schedules are possible. You may want to work a four–day week at ten hours each day. Perhaps you'll be able to spend part or all of your work week telecommuting, picking up assignments via computer modem and visiting the office two hours each week.
Your Question and Reason to Ask:

Question # 29:   Are there specific company policies I should know about?
Reason to Ask: Ask for a personnel handbook or written corporate policies. You wouldn't want to violate a policy simply because you didn't know about it.
Your Question and Reason to Ask:

Question # 30:   How are employees paid?
Reason to Ask: You'll ask this question to determine if pay arrives weekly, bi–weekly, monthly, etc.. Will you receive a physical check you have to cash, or will funds be deposited via direct deposit to your checking account? Do you want to know these things? If so, ask.
Your Question and Reason to Ask:

Question # 31:   When are you looking for someone to start?

Reason to Ask: You may use this information to help direct your campaign. The employer may expect to fill the position in a week. If so, you may want to redirect all your attentions to this coveted position. You have not wasted company time. Why should they waste your time by stretching out a job search for weeks and months?

Your Question and Reason to Ask:

Question # 32:   What do you see as some of the priorities in the department and the company over the next year?

Reason to Ask: If you have a better understanding of upcoming priorities you'll be able to promote strengths accordingly. If a skill is of primary importance to the employer, that skill is of primary importance to you. Simple, isn't it?

Your Question and Reason to Ask:

Question # 33:   Would you explain how you see time being spent each week on the various tasks that make up the job?

Reason to Ask: Remember, at least 50% of your waking hours will be spent at the job. If half of the time is spent not to your liking or benefit, do you want to commit at least 1000 hours a year to it? (20 hours/wk x 50 wks = 1000 hours.)

Your Question and Reason to Ask:

243

Question # 34: **What defines the best candidate for the job?**

Reason to Ask: Get them to define those qualities. Then meet and exceed every single one of them.

Your Question and Reason to Ask:

Question # 35: **Am I a serious contender for the position? If I am, shall we make plans to meet again?**

Reason to Ask: The interviewer will not want to meet you again if you're not suited for the position(or any other position she has available). Find this out now. If there is no way to be a contender, go and box in another ring.

Your Question and Reason to Ask:

Question # 36: **Is there anything else I may answer for you?**

Reason to Ask: A common courtesy question. They've asked everything they want to know. So have you. This question is a nice way to finish this portion of the interview and move on to any next stages.

Your Question and Reason to Ask:

Follow–Up Methods
(Or, How to Say "Thank You")

If you buy a shirt, a dress, a car, a washing machine or any other product on the market, what do you want? You probably want the product to wear well, to look good, to work as promised or to give you any type of comfort or satisfaction.

In almost every case, a person was involved with the transaction. What do you want from them? It doesn't happen every time a purchase is made. It doesn't happen too often with honesty and enthusiasm. Sometimes it happens with sarcasm. In the whole of purchasing experiences, it will occur, in a sincere way, less than 25% of the time. Do you know what it is?

"Thank you."

Are you familiar with how to value a customer? If not, you should come to understand how important we are as consumers and how important others are to us. When you read through the following example, realize how important you are to the economic health of many enterprises. Likewise, come to understand how other people and organizations are important to you. Consider this illustration:

Assume you've lived in an area for five years. Assume you spend $100 or more each week on groceries. And assume your area has two supermarkets, X and Z.

Now, let's consider how X and Z trained their staff.

X says to the cashiers— "Get the customers through as fast as possible. We don't like socializing and we expect you to process a certain dollar amount per hour. Or else." Y says to the cashiers— "The customer is king. If they need help, give it to them. Remember that they are what makes us survive and prosper. Customer loyalty has allowed us to give employees bonuses for three years running. Have fun out there and treat the customer as best you can. And thank you very much. You cashiers give the customers their impressions of this store and we couldn't do as well as we've done without you."

You go to X your first week upon moving into the area. You get in the checkout line, only to be told after 10 minutes of waiting that the aisle will close and you'll have to get in another line. You tell them you've got an important appointment. They tell you that's not their problem. In the other aisle, the cashier tells you an item isn't priced. "Oh my", you say. The cashier lets out a very dramatic sigh and calls for a checker. You don't bother to argue the outrageous price the checker gives to the cashier. You say thank you and the cashier says "yeah".

Next week you shop at Z. A new aisle is opened for you. The cashier says you seem in a rush. You tell them you missed an appointment from last week and that you had it re–scheduled for 10 minutes from now. The cashier calls for another bagger to help bag your groceries. The cashier smiles and wishes you luck on the rest of your day. Giving you your change, the cashier says "thanks very much for shopping with us. Take care, and I hope to see you next week."

You've been shopping with Z ever since.

Now, the quiz. What is your value to X and to Z? Is it $100? Absolutely not.

Your value comprises the 5 years of spending you've done since you've moved to the area. So what is your worth?

Supermarket X? $100.

Supermarket Z? $26,000.

This illustration shows the benefits of a great attitude. Likewise, your attitude at every situation will pay off in countless ways in the future.

Suppose you have spent time researching five companies and contacting twenty people in various fields. On your first interview, you are offered the job and accept it. How you treat those other contacts could very well have an important bearing on your success in the future.

You may have researched five companies in the same industry. Your chances of meeting people from one or more of those companies in the future is certainly possible. You may attend an industry conference. You may join a professional association. You may be politically appointed to a community action committee, only to share the stage with those you've met. Last, and perhaps most important, the job you chose may not work out and you'll want to revisit some of those same people.

For all of these reasons and more, your follow-up methods are very important. Though you may never work with any of these individuals in the future, the rules throughout this chapter still apply. Rules regarding honesty, enthusiasm and presentation, both written and visual, are crucial.

If you've followed procedures from this book, you've done the following:

1. Researched Industries
2. Researched Companies
3. Conducted Informational Interviews
4. Presented Yourself to Best Advantage at the Job Interview
5. Accepted One Job Offer; Declined Others

In each of the five procedures above, you were certain to encounter people. This may be apparent in items 3 through 5, but what of 1 and 2? If you are like many who conduct research, you probably received valuable information from the following:

1. A librarian.
2. A secretary.
3. A research assistant at a college or university.
4. A family member.
5. A friend.
6. A religious organization.
7. A professional association.

Each of these people has served as a valuable resource and they should be thanked for their efforts. In your new job, things may come up for which you are not experienced. If you've treated your contacts nicely, saying thank you at every opportunity, you will find resources available. These people may be available to support the job you have recently accepted.

Like the cover letter, your follow–up letters should abide by certain rules. In abbreviated order:

1. One page only.
2. Correct spelling and punctuation.
3. Three paragraphs, if possible.
4. Typed or by word processor.
5. Quality bond paper.
6. An easy to read format.

The primary difference between the cover letter and follow–up letters is in what you are selling. With cover letters, you're selling the ways you would contribute to a company. With follow–ups, you're selling companies and support people on <u>themselves</u>.

We'll break down each of the three paragraphs for cover letters and follow–ups so that you'll understand your responsibilities:

Cover Letter	Follow-Up Letter
1. Introduction	1. Introduction
You'll tell how you came to know of the job opportunity, naming advertisements and people as warranted.	You'll remind the person who you are. This includes when and where you met and under what circumstances.
2. Highlights of Qualifications	2. The Thank You
You'll match every need from the job description with your skills and abilities.	You'll tell the person how they helped you. Give examples of your strengths and how they were supported and defined.
3. Closing Statement	3. Closing Statement
You'll initiate the next step. You'll call at a specific time to set up a meeting.	You'll initiate the next step. You'll tell them that they'll be a valuable resource to future efforts.

Sometimes, writing follow-up letters to those other than job prospects seems difficult. You may find it easier to thank someone who has offered you a job than to your friendly librarian. Since the librarian and others are so vitally important to you, we'll give examples of follow-up letters to this support group.

Don't copy the letters. Instead, use them to remind yourself just how beneficial these people have been to you. Then, express your sincere gratitude to them as best you can and in your own language. However you do it, thank these people.

Friend or Relative

Your Street Address
City, State, Zip Code
Telephone Number

Date

Their Name
Title, if appropriate
Company Name, if appropriate
Street Address
City, State, Zip Code

Salutation:

How nice it is to have a favorite aunt who'll help her nephew in his job search! What an added benefit that you know so much about the concession business as it applies to a mall.

Aunt Sarah, I've been wanting to invest the money I have as best as possible. I want to be conservative in the way I handle these funds. Whereas before I considered the concession business fun but highly speculative, you've shown me that detailed planning will make this a profitable and conservative enterprise.

I'm going to rely on your expertise as I explore this field. You've always had my best interests at heart. So often we take the help of relatives for granted, but I want you to know that you have been and will be one of the biggest reasons for my success.

With much love,

Your Name

A Librarian

Your Street Address
City, State, Zip Code
Telephone Number

Date

Their Name
Title, if appropriate
Company Name, if appropriate
Street Address
City, State, Zip Code

Salutation:

Last week, I asked for your help in my efforts . I am researching the computer field in our area. Your assistance was most valuable.

As you may recall, I am considering a career change. I've been working in the retail field for many years selling apparel. I plan on transferring my skills to computer sales.

The material you suggested has really helped me. I have already made two new leads based on your suggestions. I look forward to your assistance in the future as I explore this career change further.

Sincerely,

Your Name

Professional Association

> Your Street Address
> City, State, Zip Code
> Telephone Number
>
> Date

Their Name
Title, if appropriate
Company Name, if appropriate
Street Address
City, State, Zip Code

Salutation:

I'm so glad I got the chance to meet you this week. For years now, I've been impressed with your efforts to advance the cause of fellow members of the Builders Association. It is a pleasure to know you'll help me as well.

I've done the research you suggested. So far, I've been able to meet with Mr. Green and I plan to meet with the others you suggested in the next two weeks. I've been able to learn a great deal in such a short period of time. Still, though, I find new questions coming to mind.

I would very much appreciate meeting with you again. I do not think I'd need more than twenty minutes of your time. I've attached a sheet which lists the 8 questions I now have. Your observations would be very valuable.

I'll call you on Tuesday. I look forward to meeting with you soon.

> Sincerely,
>
> Your Name

Prospective Employer

Your Street Address
City, State, Zip Code
Telephone Number

Date

Their Name
Title, if appropriate
Company Name, if appropriate
Street Address
City, State, Zip Code

Salutation:

On Tuesday, we met to discuss your open position for Legal Secretary.

I was very impressed with your firm. The methods you employ to maintain the highest quality from all employees is admirable. I felt a high degree of dedication from all your staff and was glad to see that everyone wanted to contribute to overall company success.

I'm sure I would contribute to this environment. The skills I would bring to the job are sure to complement the skills of others. I've already thought of a way to enhance the communications systems in the office to allow for 24–hour customer service.

I will call you next week on Monday to learn of where you're at in the decision–making process. Of course, you are welcome to call me at any time.

Sincerely,

Your Name

Religious Organization

Your Street Address
City, State, Zip Code
Telephone Number

Date

Their Name
Title, if appropriate
Organization Name, if appropriate
Street Address
City, State, Zip Code

Salutation:

I came to you last week to seek guidance on my job search.

For years now, I've attended your services. You've provided me with the inspirations needed to conduct a fulfilling personal life. Only upon meeting with you personally, though, did I realize that much of the same inspiration in my personal life can be directed towards professional goals.

I was encouraged by your suggestions. I'm very pleased that you'll be speaking with Mrs. Gonic next week. I would very much like to meet her and discuss my future plans. Her insights are sure to be as welcome as your own.

Thanks again for all your help. I'll let you know of my progress after your service this Sunday. I look forward to it.

Sincerely,

Your Name

A Research Assistant

Your Street Address
City, State, Zip Code
Telephone Number

Date

Their Name
Title, if appropriate
Company Name, if appropriate
Street Address
City, State, Zip Code

Salutation:

Last week, you helped me locate the many resource materials I needed for my job search.

I am determined to be successful in architectural design. I was fully aware of the market in Phoenix. You showed me many valuable ways to explore the field in Boston. I plan to meet with all the people you mentioned. I'm sure I'll be able to meet all of them over the next two weeks.

Though I've just moved to the area, your help assures me of a promising future in this community.

Thank you very much.

Sincerely,

Your Name

A Secretary

> Your Street Address
> City, State, Zip Code
> Telephone Number
>
> Date

Their Name
Title, if appropriate
Company Name, if appropriate
Street Address
City, State, Zip Code

Salutation:

Recently, I visited your department looking for information on the marketing field in publishing. You were very helpful with your suggestions.

I have followed through on your leads. The company library you suggested was full with information. I've also scheduled an informational meeting with Mrs. Saunderson at the Cabot Company. She was most pleased to hear that you consider her a valuable resource.

I will let you know how I've progressed over the next couple of months. You've helped me a great deal and I thank you.

> Best regards,
>
> Your Name

Turning Down an Offer

Your Street Address
City, State, Zip Code
Telephone Number

Date

Their Name
Title, if appropriate
Company Name, if appropriate
Street Address
City, State, Zip Code

Salutation:

After contributing four years to Albot Corporation, I have decided to accept a position with The Hanover Group.

The Hanover Group offers challenges in both marketing analysis and client relations. My skills with computer–enhanced imaging analysis and developing in–house training programs will prove equally valuable to my new employer and client base.

I appreciate your considering me for the position and making me a job offer. Though I have accepted another position, I am grateful for your interest in me and the contributions I would have made to your organization.

My best regards to you and your firm.

Sincerely,

Your Name

So They Want You—Now What?
(Or, Weighing the Job Offer)

You've been offered a job. Is it a great job? Is it a good job? What did you think about the people in the office that moment you walked through the door? Were there clients in the office? What did you think of them? Now, answer the most important question:

How did you feel about the whole thing as you went through the process and then left the interview?

Some people have that 'gut feeling'. That feeling tells them if an offer is right or wrong for them. Other people simply say they 'know' the offer is good for them. Whichever way you consider the offer, you must only have your interests at heart.

You, as an individual, can have immediate, truthful reactions to a situation if you've done your research thoroughly. That 'gut feeling' comes from the knowledge that ones needs in a job will be met or unmet. Without the proper research, the best offers will be met with tentative apprehension at best.

Know what you want. Know what you want to give. Know what the company will offer, in every respect. You'll then know if the offer is good or bad. For you.

Again, The Salary Question

Through your research of the company you have a good idea of the salary range for a position. Therefore, you have no reason to inquire about salary yourself. Furthermore, you should not talk about salary during your first interview. As you have discovered during your research, a job is important to you for so many reasons. The take–home pay, the pension, vacations, medical benefits, commuting hours, flexible work hours, etc. will all play a part in your decision. Your first interview will only validate your interest in the position and in the company.

Your current and previous salary history has absolutely no direct bearing on your potential position. Remember that. The only reason a prospective employer wants to know salary information is to use it against you as a bargaining tool. Remember that too. In every case, do not reveal salary information.

Consider what you should earn with the new employer. You've analyzed the position. You know what you need to earn to support yourself. Treat salary negotiations as a game. A poker game. Just as in a poker game, those that give away their hand lose. So too with your salary. Work off their hand, not the other way around.

You may feel uncomfortable thinking of salary negotiations in terms of gamesmanship. But understand that if you're high–strung about every dollar bargained, the employer will sense your concern. Then, the employer will hammer away at every portion of the negotiation, taking instead of giving at each turn.

Responding to the Figure Offered

As hard as it seems, you must pause when given an offer(in dollars). You may be working for six months, a year or more before you'll get a raise. Therefore, treat your response as one of the most important events that will happen in your life for some time to come. It is.

When the offer is made, pause for a moment and look down at the ground or at your feet. Think about the offer and think about something really, really bad that has happened to you. Perhaps a failed exam, the death of a family pet, etc.. After this 'very pregnant pause', look at the interviewer. Maintain eye to eye contact and ask "Is that the best offer you're able to make?".

If the answer to your question is yes, you thank them and say you'll need a day to come to your decision. You will need this day to fill out your Compensation Chart. A seemingly great offer may need some adjustments after you've had some time to consider it further. If further negotiations are necessary, one day will give you the clarity needed to present your demands to the employer.

If the offer is not final, you'll immediately want to reiterate the great qualities you'll bring to the job. You do not want to allow the employer to ask "Well, what do you want?". Ask what the salary range is for the job being offered. Depending on where in that range your offer is, you may judge how best to negotiate.

Large corporations have established ranges for all positions. Small firms may actually offer more of a spread between the first offer and subsequent terms. With a small firm, you should explain exactly why you are so crucially important to the success of their firm. Point out the added skills you have that are so vital to a progressive company. The small firm will always be concerned that they are keeping up with other firms in their industry. Their perception of you will determine how much they'll be willing to pay.

When you form an opinion about people on television, do you really know everything about them? What you perceive forms your opinions. Similarly, let the employer think of you as the best and only choice for the position. Then, write your own ticket.

Compensation

We'll look at a simple example of compensation to highlight the need for full analysis of any dollars offered.

Suppose your paycheck totals $30,000 per year. Is that your compensation? Absolutely not. So many other components may affect your standard of living. You must consider all aspects of compensation before deciding whether or not an offer is attractive to you.

If you earn $30,000 and pay your own medical insurance are you better off than someone who earns $29,000 and has medical insurance included? What if medical insurance costs $2,000 per year. Without allowing for tax implications, we have:

Job Now	**Job Offer**
$30,000 Pay Minus $2,000 Medical	$29,000 Pay Plus $2,000 Medical
$28,000 Net Compensation	$31,000 Total Compensation

Don't be fooled into thinking you are $3,000 ahead with the job offer. You're not. Accepting the offer, though, you'd be raising your compensation by $1,000. Perhaps you're covered under a spouses medical plan. In that case, you may find you'd actually be earning more with your current job($30,000 vs. $29,000). The most important thing for you to understand is that your negotiations apply to you only. What the company pays somebody else has absolutely no bearing on you. If you are told what others make in the position, explain how unique you are. You are unique. Be rewarded for that uniqueness.

To figure how attractive a job offer really is, you should first analyze your total compensation at present. You know how the pay you receive now affects your life. Even if you earn no money, fill out the Current Compensation Chart. You'll find values that are important to you that do not translate into a dollar figure.

Perhaps you're a recently divorced woman. You've not had a job in ten years. Fill out the charts. Maybe the sales position you want will provide a company car, saving you the $280 monthly car payment you now pay yourself. And what if you can net $5,000 from the car you now have by selling it? Would a company car, $5,000 in the bank and $262.50 in simple 5 1/4% interest(yearly) help you?

Weigh the importance of each item on the compensation sheets. Arrive at a decision that benefits you the most. Be as exact as possible. You do not want to think less of an offer only to find your attitude was based on assumptions that weren't true.

Yes, money is what pays the bills and puts food on the table. Weigh that take–home pay accordingly. Still, remember that so much more affects your happiness.

Also, remember that each and every company is a unique institution. Some may state a salary figure from which they won't budge. Others will raise their offers 2 or more times. With some, your refusal to give the exact dollar figures for your salary history(for the last 15 years!) will put you out of the running. You have to decide on all things important to your job search and stick to them.

The Pep Talk

If you've gone to 20 interviews and have been turned down for every job, repeat the following statement:

"I may not get a job until the 100th interview. Isn't that 100th company lucky to move into 1st place because they hired me!" The quote may seem a bit sappy, but you must consider yourself the most important asset throughout the whole job search process.

The charts on the following pages will allow you to compare current and prospective dollar and compensation values. Use them fully. Don't discount anything. Your future happiness is at stake.

Current Compensation

1.   Your current yearly gross salary is   :_____
2.   Are there bonuses you may be assured of   :_____
3.   Are there stock options you can value   :_____
4.   What contributions will your employer
     make towards your pension plan   :_____
5.   What profit sharing do you receive   :_____
6.   What commissions do you receive   :_____
7.   Do you get an expense account   :_____
8.   Have you received paid reimbursement
     for schooling   :_____
9.   What medical insurance do you receive   :_____
10. Dental insurance   :_____
11. Life insurance   :_____
12. Disability insurance   :_____
13. Do you get a company car   :_____
14. Do you use low–interest company loans?
     If so, how much do you save by using these
     loans versus a regular bank   :_____
15. If you leave your job, do you receive
     a severance package   :_____
16. Are there miscellaneous items that you
     receive for which you can assign value?
     If so, list them and assign a value.

                         Item   :_____
                         Item   :_____
                         Item   :_____
                         Item   :_____
                         Item   :_____

                 Total Compensation:_____

     Finally, some of these values are more important to you
than others. You've got to weigh each item individually when
determining if this job best suits your needs.

Job Offer Compensation

1. The yearly gross salary offer is :_____
2. What bonuses you may be assured of :_____
3. Are there stock options you can value :_____
4. What contributions will your employer
   make towards your pension plan :_____
5. What profit sharing will you receive :_____
6. What commissions will you receive :_____
7. Do you get an expense account :_____
8. Will you receive paid reimbursement
   for schooling :_____
9. What medical insurance will you receive :_____
10. Dental insurance :_____
11. Life insurance :_____
12. Disability insurance :_____
13. Will you get a company car :_____
14. Will you use low–interest company loans?
    If so, how much will you save by using these
    loans versus a regular bank :_____
15. If you lost this job after working as long as on
    your current job, what would your severance
    package be: :_____
16. Are there miscellaneous items that you
    would get for which you can assign value?
    If so, list them and assign a value.

    Item :_____
    Item :_____
    Item :_____
    Item :_____

    Total Compensation:_____

Remember, some of these values are more important to
you than others. Therefore, weigh each item individually when
determining if the job would best suit your needs.

Worksheets

Many people write lists every day or every week. These lists may be for groceries, for appointments, for yourself or for others. You can write a list to make note of anything.

Like the lists, worksheets enable you to set a course of action and follow that course however precisely you wish. Worsheets may determine your rate of success or failure.

Visually, you may use any means to follow your progress. A worksheet, chart or list may work best for you. As items are completed, you may use a highlighter or black marker to cross an item off your list. Use a check mark. Make notes next to the item under consideration. When you revise a list, transfer unfinished work and any notes you've written over to your next document. And so on.

Do you know these documents are just as important as the written laws and contracts that govern our lives? The answer lies in how obligated we feel when something(a contract) or someone(with a contract in hand) shows us what we've agreed to at an earlier date. There is no denial possible. We can argue to make future amendments, but we have to acknowledge the existence of the document.

Use this process for yourself. Lists, worksheets, charts or any other written methods will help you in countless ways. You'll be able to track how you spend your time, who you've contacted, what responses you've received, where you've done research and why you've succeeded every step of the way.

Use the worksheets in this book. You may decide to modify them as you wish. Whatever you do, use them. The worksheets are a viable, concrete method to meet with success.

Action Verbs

Analyzed, assisted, administered, advised, arranged, acquired, audited, assembled, attained, authored, acted, approved, assessed

Built, balanced, budgeted

Created, completed, consulted, calculated, contracted, controlled, conducted, compounded, consolidated, counseled, coordinated, collected, charted

Designed, delivered, diagnosed, dispensed, dispersed, detected, distributed, disproved, developed, directed, determined, drew, devised, discovered

Evaluated, examined, edited, eliminated, expanded, executed, enlisted, expedited, established, educated

Founded, formulated, facilitated, forecasted, fashioned, familiarized

Guided, grew, generated

Held, headed

Instructed, identified, increased, improved, invented, installed, implemented, instituted, interpreted, interviewed, increased, initiated

Joined

Leveraged, lectured, logged, launched

Maintained, managed, mediated, moderated, marketed, motivated, monitored

Negotiated, networked

Action Verbs (Cont'd)

Observed, ordered, obtained, oversaw, operated, organized, overhauled, originated

Planned, performed, produced, processed, protected, programmed, purchased, presented, provided, prescribed, promoted, prepared

Reduced, restored, referred, reviewed, rendered, received, recommended, realized, rewarded, researched, represented

Sold, supplied, served, studied, selected, solved, supervised, strategized, scheduled, strengthened, systematized, screened

Trained, tested, translated, tabulated, transformed, trimmed, tripled

Upgraded, uncovered, unraveled

Viewed, validated

Wrote, won

Company Research Plan

Company Name:
Company Address:
Telephone Number:

Possible Contacts at Company:

Name:
Title:
Address:
Phone:

Name:
Title:
Address:
Phone:

	1988	1989	1990	1991
Company Yearly Sales				
Company Yearly Net Profit				

Credit Rating
Total Employees

Name of Chairman
Name of President
Name of Owner
Senior Person in Your Area of Interest

General Background of Company(i.e. Year Founded, Primary Businesses, etc.):

Research Findings on Your Area of Interest:

Related Departments:

Current Compensation

1. Your current yearly gross salary is :_____
2. Are there bonuses you may be assured of :_____
3. Are there stock options you can value :_____
4. What contributions will your employer make towards your pension plan :_____
5. What profit sharing do you receive :_____
6. What commissions do you receive :_____
7. Do you get an expense account :_____
8. Have you received paid reimbursement for schooling :_____
9. What medical insurance do you receive :_____
10. Dental insurance :_____
11. Life insurance :_____
12. Disability insurance :_____
13. Do you get a company car :_____
14. Do you use low–interest company loans? If so, how much do you save by using these loans versus a regular bank :_____
15. If you leave your job, do you receive a severance package :_____
16. Are there miscellaneous items that you receive for which you can assign value? If so, list them and assign a value.

    Item :_____
    Item :_____
    Item :_____
    Item :_____

    Total Compensation :_____

Finally, some of these values are more important to you than others. You've got to weigh each item individually when determining if this job best suits your needs.

Job Offer Compensation

1. The yearly gross salary offer is   :_____
2. What bonuses you may be assured of   :_____
3. Are there stock options you can value   :_____
4. What contributions will your employer
    make towards your pension plan   :_____
5. What profit sharing will you receive   :_____
6. What commissions will you receive   :_____
7. Do you get an expense account   :_____
8. Will you receive paid reimbursement
    for schooling   :_____
9. What medical insurance will you receive   :_____
10. Dental insurance   :_____
11. Life insurance   :_____
12. Disability insurance   :_____
13. Will you get a company car   :_____
14. Will you use low–interest company loans?
    If so, how much will you save by using these
    loans versus a regular bank   :_____
15. If you lost this job after working as long as on
    your current job, what would your severance
    package be: :_____
16. Are there miscellaneous items that you
    would get for which you can assign value?
    If so, list them and assign a value.

> Item   :_____
> Item   :_____
> Item   :_____
> Item   :_____
>
> Total Compensation   :_____

Remember, some of these values are more important to you than others. Therefore, weigh each item individually when determining if the job would best suit your needs.

Planning Schedule

Week Number:____From:_____To:_____
               (Include Day and Date)   (Day and Date)

Hours   Hours
I'll Spend: I've Accomplished:

_____   Researching Industries   _____

_____   Researching Companies   _____

_____   Contacting People   _____

_____   Refining My Résumé   _____

_____   Improving My Skills   _____

_____   Getting Informational Interviews   _____

_____   Having Informational Interviews   _____

_____   Following–Up Leads   _____

_____   Answer Job Advertisements   _____

_____   Having Job Interviews   _____

_____   Using Agencies(Temp, etc.)   _____

_____   Planning Activities for Next Week   _____

_____   Reading Self–Help Books   _____

_____   Learning Something New   _____

Total Hours Planned Planned: ____Total Hours Completed:_____

Following Through on the Job Prospect

Contact Name:
Title:
Company Name:
Address:
Phone:

Cover Letter Sent?	Yes	No	Date(s):
Résumé Attached?	Yes	No	Date(s):
Résumé Sent Alone?	Yes	No	Date(s):

Follow–Up Phone Call?	Yes	No	Date:

Phone #:
Spoke With:
Time:

Interview Set?	Yes	No	Date:

With Whom:
Location:
Time:
Phone #:

Are You Prepared With

6 Copies of Résumé?	Yes	No	
Pressed Clothing?	Yes	No	
Grooming?	Yes	No	
Travel Plans?	Yes	No	What?
A Practice Interview?	Yes	No	
Any Exceteras?	Yes	No	What?

Post–Interview,

Was An Offer Made?	Yes	No

If yes, has Compensation

Chart been filled out?	Yes	No
Thank–You Letters Sent?	Yes	No

Agencies, Recruiters, etc.

You've worked very hard at getting information and material through research. You've identified your qualifications and the contributions you will make to an organization. You have taken control of your job search. Likewise, when using outside agencies to support your efforts, you must take control.

There's the story of a man who was trying to get a job during tough economic times. We'd learned how he was going about his job search. We expected to be impressed. He'd been a highly regarded executive all of his life. He knew his skills were outstanding.

First we learned that he'd been unemployed for thirteen months! Through our investigation we learned why. Primarily, he wanted a job to come to him. He put out great efforts. Still, he gave the responsibilities to the employers.

We found that he tried to find employment by sending out over 1000 résumés to companies all over the country. Over 1000! Of course, by now you understand why this method was a terrible mistake. You would have to conduct research on almost 20 companies per week, every week, in order to cover those 1000 firms in a year. Either this man was extremely educated on vast numbers of companies or totally lost in his personal paperwork(try writing cover letters and printing and mailing résumés to 1000 employers). With thirteen months of unemployment this man proved he was lost.

If you look at the efforts you put forth through previous chapters of this book, you'll realize that you have taken control.

You've researched an industry. you've chosen a group of progressive companies. And you've determined why those companies need you. The man in our example hasn't determined anything. (Actually, he may have learned that he would be able to work well as a file clerk.)

Now, if you use any type of agency, take control. Remember that any agency is providing you with a service. They are in business for you. Don't forget that.

If you work for a temporary agency, in most cases the agency will receive a certain dollar amount on top of your hourly salary *for every hour you work*. If you work as a consultant for an agency, the same situation most likely occurs. Headhunters will most probably earn percentages of the annual salaries of the people they place. Since you are giving them so much for placing you, shouldn't you be placed where you'd be benefited most?

The Rules

When you walk into the permanent placement agency, you'll want to(and must) accomplish the following:

1. Make them understand you'll work with one representative only. You will not be passed around the office.

2. Ask the agency to provide you with written documentation about their company. Use this information to decide if you should work with this agency or move on. If no written documentation exists, you'll want to learn:

   • How long has the agency been in business?
   • How many clients do they represent?
   • Are they experienced in placing people in your field of interest?
   • How long does it typically take to place people?
   • Do they have anything in writing that highlights the services they'll provide to you?

- Are there any fees you'll be expected to pay?(If there are fees, get out of that agency! You should never have to pay to use your skills and make your contributions. Period.)

3. Determine the quality of the individual you'll be working with at the agency. Find answers to the following:

- How long have they been with the agency?
- How does their success at placing people compare with others in the office?
- How many people comprise their workload?
- Is this individual familiar with the industries you're interested in? If not, is there someone better suited to your needs?
- How will this person keep in contact with you throughout the process? When you leave a short–term position, will you have to push this person for additional work assignments?

Think about what is important to you and ask away!

You'll be providing these people with your résumé. As with everything else in your job search, you'll want to control how the agency uses this important document. You will:

1. Let them know immediately that you'll be maintaining control over how your résumé is distributed. You do not want to mimic our earlier example and find 1000 copies of your résumé littering the streets with your qualifications. Make known the following:

- Identify an industry or industries you want to pursue.
- Identify the companies that impress you.
- Set rules for how they'll approach your market. For example, allow them to send out résumés to 5 companies in each of 3 industries. If they are doing their job, 15 résumés will make for a constructive beginning.

Again, make sure that the agency understands your role will be proactive, not reactive. Tell them you'll be continuing your research, that you'll support them as best you can and that you'll expect them to be working diligently for you.

Temporary Assignments

You may want to consider working for a temporary agency as a 'temp'. Jobs offered by these agencies may last a day or a few days. Or, you may find work that lasts weeks, months or even a full year.

If you decide to follow this route, do not accept job assignments only according to length of assignment and pay per hour. By this time you should know why.

Temporary assignments provide one of the best methods for research. You can develop a better understanding of certain products being sold. You may get a sense of job satisfaction from full–time employees. You may decide whether or not you like the environment the industry or typical company provides to workers. You'll also get a sense of how to sell yourself to that industry and how skilled people move up in the organization.

Use careful consideration when choosing an agency. Remember, each time they place you, each hour you work, they'll receive a fee from the company who has hired you. They may earn two to ten dollars per hour, or more. Expect that they'll want to place you very quickly.

Therefore, you must do preliminary research on the industries you want to get involved with. Make your interest known to the agency. Say no to assignments that are not in your best interests. You may favor the agency by working for a short period for a company that does not interest you. If so, make the agency understand that you want another assignment and give them an ending date for the current assignment.

When working as a temporary in a company, volunteer to do anything for that company. Try to find new things you'd like to

280

learn and offer to be trained. Offer to work overtime(negotiated at a minimum 1 1/2 times normal hourly rate, of course).

If you are doing a great deal more than when first hired for the assignment, consider two options. First, decide if the work interests you enough, and will pay you enough, to offer your services as a full-time employee. Or, if you're not interested in full-time but are doing a lot more than required initially, ask your agency(not the company) to renegotiate your pay.

If a job offer is made to you, the employer may be expected to pay the agency to buy your contract. After all, when the agency loses your services, they lose profit on you by the hour!(That should remind you how important you are.) In every case, do not accept lower pay or benefits simply because your new employer had to spend some up-front money to get you. Simply explain that paying for quality(you) assures that company of their success in the future.

Never expect an employer or agency to raise your pay on their own initiative. Whether you have a formal review process or walk into the boss demanding more money, your actions alone will get you more money and rewards.

Finally, do not assume that temporary assignments benefit only one segment of the working population. This assumption is not true. Everyone may benefit from these types of assignments. Temporaries have been found at all levels, from file clerks to the CEO of a major corporation. Does your job category fall somewhere between the two?

Conclusion

You've journeyed a long way towards achieving career goals. The instructions, the guidelines and the rules in this book have set the stage for your self–analysis.

If you've read the whole book and have done the exercises throughout, you've spent many days or weeks getting prepared for a better future. I thank you for the time you have given to this book.

Remember that no method offers a 100% guarantee for a designated success. Do you recall our mentioning having "gut feelings" about a situation? You'll know what feels right for you. If that "gut feeling" tells you to take certain paths listen to that internal message. You've received great advice, now put it to work as best benefits your personal situation.

I wish you every success, whatever path you choose to follow.

You must always remember to:

- Analyze your needs.

- Research as much as possible.

- Be prepared for all encounters.

- Smile and say thank you to everyone you meet.

- Keep a written record of everything you do and that needs to be done.

- Improve yourself at every opportunity.

- Always have goals.

- Define your own success.

- Prosper in your life.

If you have faith in yourself and what you can do in life, only you will set your limits. Know no boundaries and aim high!

Index

Historians 50
History 119
Hobbies 11, 12, 36, 90, 94, 95
Homeowners 50
Honesty 46, 175, 176, 245, 247
Honors 101
Hospital 16
Hotel industry 109
Housing development agency 5

Identify successes 22
Imagined people 41
Impending layoff 17
Importance of style 185
Industry 59
Industry worksheet 50
Inequalities 99
Informal market 2
Information society 47, 99
Informational interviews 15, 52, 53, 59, 60, 62, 247
Insurance 109
Integrity 231
Integrity of references 165
Interaction 46
Intern 101
International shipping 5
Interview 3, 4, 5, 13, 15, 35, 47, 48, 53, 60, 62, 115, 154, 160, 174, 178, 179, 185, 186, 247, 260
Interview questions 5, 177
Interviewer 41, 48, 50, 60, 161, 164, 165, 177, 179, 180, 184, 185, 186, 187, 231, 232
Interviewers' assessment 163
Interviewing 91
Investigator 96
Investment ratings books 52

Jargon 101
Jewelry 170, 171
Job assignments 280
Job blocks 117
Job changes 9

Order Form

To order additional copies of The Smart Job Search or any of the other titles listed below, simply fill out this order form and return it to us for quick shipment. Remember, all books offer a 30–day money–back guarantee.

Title	Quantity	x Price	= Total
The Smart Job Search— **A Guide to Proven Methods** for Finding a Great Job ISBN 0–9630394–8–2	_____	x $18.95	= _____
Résumés for **The Smart Job Search** ISBN 0–9630394–9–0 Publication Date: January 1992	_____	x $14.95	= _____

Smart Smart Smart
Quarterly Newsletter published by the author of The Smart Job Search. Mr. Makos offers timely advice focusing on career development. Interviews are included in each issue.

Single Issue @ $4: _____

One Year(4 issues) @ $8: _____

Sub-Total: _____

Shipping: Please add $2.50/first book delivery, $1.00/each book thereafter. NO SHIPPING CHARGES on newsletters. : _____

Massachusetts residents must add 5% sales tax: : _____

Total Order: _____

Your Name:_____

Address:_____

City, State, ZIP:_____

Daytime Telephone:_____

Please mail check or money order to: **HD Publishing** **P.O. Box 2171-TSJS** **Boston, MA 02106**